THE MAKING OF

Schindler's List

THE MAKING OF

Schindler's List

BEHIND THE SCENES OF AN EPIC FILM

Franciszek Palowski

Translated from the Polish by Anna and Robert G. Ware

A BIRCH LANE PRESS BOOK

Published by Carol Publishing Group

A Birch Lane Press Book
Published by Carol Publishing Group
Birch Lane Press is a registered trademark of Carol Communications, Inc.

Editorial, sales and distribution, rights and permissions inquiries should be addressed
to Carol Publishing Group, 120 Enterprise Avenue, Secaucus, N.J. 07094.

In Canada: Canadian Manda Group, One Atlantic Avenue, Suite 105, Toronto,
Ontario, M6K 3E7

Carol Publishing Group books may be purchased in bulk at special discounts for sales
promotion, fund-raising, or educational purposes. Special editions can be created to
specifications. For details, contact Special Sales Department, Carol Publishing Group,
120 Enterprise Avenue, Secaucus, N.J. 07094.

Manufactured in the United States of America
10 9 8 7 6 5 4 3 2 1

Library of Congress Cataloging-in-Publication Data

Palowski, Franciszek, 1942–
    [Spielberg w poszukiwaniu Arki. English]
    The making of Schindler's list: behind the scenes of an epic film
/ Franciszek Palowski ; translated from the Polish by Anna and
Robert G. Ware.
        p.   cm.
    "A Birch Lane Press book."
    ISBN 1–55972–445–5 (hc.)
    1. Schindler's list (Motion picture)   I. Title.
PN1997.S3133P3613   1998
791.43'72—dc21
                                                97–41443
                                                    CIP

To my mother

Whoever saves one life, saves the world entire.

The Talmud

CONTENTS

PREFACE

This book is at times a chronicle, at times a diary—a personal observation, and an appreciation of the making of *Schindler's List*. Published in Poland before the film was released, it witnesses the process of making a work of cinema about a comparatively recent series of factual events. The uniqueness of Steven Spielberg's achievement is that he managed to capture history in a form that compels the interest of his audience and in some sense might even be said to "entertain." In contrast to his more recent films, *Schindler's List* was managed on a small budget, in black-and-white, and with restrained spectacle. Seldom in today's world of media frenzy, glitter, and excess do we find an artist with the courage to follow the axiom that "less is more." In *Schindler's List*, Spielberg makes economy and control of every resource a cinematic virtue and an artistic asset. This book allows us to become intimate with some of his process and his inspiration.

Nearly thirty thousand people worked on the realization of this film. Often the conditions were far from ideal: brutally cold and adverse weather, laborious distances, and extreme hours. This book is a testimony to the remarkable capability of the Polish people today as well as a chronicle of the international collaboration required to support the achievement of Steven Spielberg's vision. Finally, the book also contributes to our better understanding and appreciation of those people whose story is the story of *Schindler's List*.

My wife, Anna, is a native of Kraków, Poland, and a survivor
of the Auschwitz-Birkenau and Bergen-Belsen camps. For several years we traveled each summer to Kraków where we
enjoyed returning to the place of her childhood and the
wonderfully relaxed medieval quality of the Old City. In 1994,
we had, of course, seen *Schindler's List,* so when we saw a book,
Spielberg: In Search of the Ark, in a shop on Szeroka Square—part
of the old Jewish section of the city—we had to buy it. That
night Anna started reading and could not put it down. She
translated aloud to me about filming the sequence of the Jewish
exodus across the bridge to the ghetto. I, too, was fascinated,
and moved. We arranged for a friend to introduce us to
Franciszek Palowski, its author. He met us in the cafe Jama
Michalika (Michael's Cave), and there we tried to convince the
author that the book must be shared by more than just those in
the world who read Polish. Before our tea was finished, we
realized that what we should do was translate the text and
develop an English edition. It became a mission—to offer the
opportunity for English readers to become familiar with the
making of Spielberg's extraordinary film.

Franciszek Palowski is a distinguished Polish journalist, television personality, and teacher. He witnessed Steven Spielberg's
work on *Schindler's List* from the first moment the director set
foot on Polish soil to begin planning the film. A humanist and
scholar, Mr. Palowski's understanding of European history as
well as his regard for his countrymen's experience of World War
II has lead him to a broad range of contacts and friendships—
Gentile and Jew—among his countrymen and throughout Europe. It was this background and his facility in English that
made Mr. Palowski able to aid Steven Spielberg as a consultant
and interpreter. This book is a product of his interesting
relationship to the making of the film.

The point of view of the book assumes a knowledge of Jewish
customs, Polish history, and the unique characteristics of
Kraków and its environs. We have added footnotes for readers
unfamiliar with these matters where an insertion into the text
would intrude. An interesting aspect of the book is that it was

written and published before the film of *Schindler's List* was
released. Its author knew nothing of the final cut of the film or
how it would succeed before audiences. We have added an
epilogue to the original text, as well as footnotes that endeavor
to link the original text to the present—four years later—and
assess Spielberg's achievement in the context of the present.
Information about the principals in the *Schindler's List* film has
been updated through the footnotes as well. All footnotes are
additions by us to the original text.

In developing this English version there are certain conventions we have employed. Brackets [ ] in the text signal our
insertions within the original book. Contractions have been
used where they help to sustain the informal, conversational, or
"diary" quality of the original. Much of the text is in the first
person because that is the voice of the author—an oral narra-
tive. A compelling characteristic of Franciszek Palowski's original book is the way he uses these devices of the first person and
the present tense to engage the reader in the project, as if he or
she were present for the actual events. We have sought to
sustain this quality in our English text.

We are particularly grateful to our colleague, George Diestel,
Ph.D., for his suggestions and his expertise as a scholar of
religion and of the Holocaust. Our thanks to Ryszard and Maria
Hodur of Kraków, Poland, who arranged for us to meet
Franciszek Palowski. Our thanks also to our son, Robert E.
Levin, for his advice and encouragement, to Amelia Hernandez
for reading the manuscript, and to Susan and Chester Neville's
"The Laser's Edge" for access to the laser discs we needed to
verify data. We are grateful to Leopold "Poldek" Page, through
whose efforts the memory of the righteous deeds of Oscar
Schindler has been preserved, and to Irving Glovin for his
valuable advice as we were giving our manuscript its final form.
Finally, we are especially thankful to Allan J. Wilson of the
Carol Publishing Group for his patience and support.

ON MAKING THE FILM

I had the rights to make *Schindler's List* in 1982. I didn't go to work on it right away because I didn't know *how* to do it. The story didn't have the same shape as the other films I have made. It is certainly not an entertaining story in the way I make entertainment. It was something that didn't come naturally for me. I also needed time to mature within myself and develop my own consciousness about the Holocaust. I had to wait until a time when I really felt that I was ready to express myself on the subject of Oskar Schindler and make a very serious movie about his life and deeds.

I feel more like a journalist than a director of this movie. I feel like I'm reporting more than creating. These events, the character of Oskar Schindler, and the good deeds he did at a terrible time weren't created by me, they were created by history. I'm rather interpreting history, trying to find a way of communicating that history to people, but I'm not really using the strengths that I usually use to entertain people. I have a very strong urge to entertain, to keep the audience interested—not to bore anybody. Now, to make this movie, I am using a completely different set of tools that, as a filmmaker, I never really had my hands on before. This film is not supposed to please an audience—bring the audience to an exciting, adventurous conclusion. Life is not a film. In this sense, this film resembles life much more than life would remind one of film.

Steven Spielberg
—from a televised interview with the author

THE MAKING OF

Schindler's List

1

Close Encounters

Sunday morning Poldek Page called from Los Angeles. Seven
A.M.—the hour was ungodly. Not long before, I had returned
from a birthday party at some friend's house, but the news from
across the ocean made me jump to my feet: Steven Spielberg
will arrive on Tuesday. He wants to make a film about Oskar
Schindler in Kraków.

Poldek's voice in the receiver sounded very matter-of-fact: "I
showed him tapes from the television programs we did together,
your articles, and I gave him your phone number. I cannot
accompany him, so I would like you to show him Kraków.
Spielberg wants personally—with his own hands—to touch the
authentic places in Kraków where the history of Schindler and
his Jews played itself out."

I had to promise Poldek absolute secrecy. This was a require-
ment for joining Spielberg's group.

Leopold "Poldek" Pfefferberg, who after the war changed his
name to Leopold Page, was born in the part of Kraków called
Podgórze. There he went to high school, afterwards completing
a degree at Jagiellonian University in Kraków. Then he became

a high school teacher and an officer in the Polish army. As the only second lieutenant of Jewish descent, he was selected to be one of the standard bearers for the celebrations marking the twentieth anniversary of Polish independence in 1938. During the September campaign* he was a company commander. Injured in the battle on the San River, Poldek was saved by another soldier, a Polish peasant who lifted Poldek onto his back and carried him from the battlefield. Later, Poldek was taken prisoner but managed to escape from a hospital train passing through Kraków as it transported wounded captured officers to a prison camp in Germany where friends hid him from the Gestapo. Despite all his efforts, however, Poldek never found that peasant soldier after the war.

Oskar Schindler arrived in Kraków at the beginning of September 1939. A German born in the Sudetenland in Czechoslovakia, he was a thirty-one-year-old bon vivant, wheeler-dealer, and member of the German Abwehr [the German intelligence service]. In Kraków, he began setting himself up in business. Intending to manufacture enamelware, he took over a factory on Zabłocie Street in Podgórze—a suburb of Kraków where Poldek was born. Poldek first saw Schindler when Schindler came to his mother's interior decoration shop. Poldek's instinct was to kill him—he had a small Belgian six-shooter—because he thought that the Gestapo had finally discovered his whereabouts and had come for him. Later, Poldek would discover that at that moment, in the fall of 1939, he might have killed the one man to whom he and others would owe their very lives.

That man, Oskar Schindler, transformed a struggling factory known as Rekord into the lucrative Deutsche Emailwaren Fabrik [German Enamelware Factory]. As a result, he was under

---

*In September 1939 Hitler invaded Poland. This action started World War II. The September campaign refers to the Polish effort to repel the Nazi forces. Kraków fell in one week. Warsaw held out for three.

the protection of the Wehrmacht [the German army] because his factory produced vital war materials—enamel pots. He convinced the officials of the German occupation to let him select and employ all the skilled workers he needed from among the Jews in the ghetto, or later, in the Płaszów camp.

Bribery—offering jewelry and gold—was but one means of persuasion. Other methods that he used had been known since gambling was invented. For instance, he would play cards for high stakes and then lose to the person whose protection, support, or favors he wanted. It was after one such game, when his "victims" were in his grasp, that he convinced them he should not waste manpower—a workday was twelve hours, after all—so it would be best that the Jews should not return to the camp in Płaszów but instead live in a sub-camp he would organize at the factory.

Schindler's "skilled" workers included professionals in various trades as well as artists, educators, and even five-year-old children. It was as if he wanted to preserve a representative spectrum of the Jewish culture for the future within the enclave of his factory—as if a modern Noah had selected at least one representative of each kind for his ark. Schindler's methods and influence were so successful that he was even able to "liberate" three hundred Jewish women loaded onto a train of cattle wagons sent by mistake to the Auschwitz-Birkenau* concentration camp. Poldek's wife Mila was among those women. So far as

---

*The two camps of Auschwitz and Birkenau are located three miles apart. The Auschwitz camp is characterized by brick multistory buildings, the entrance to which is through the famous overarching iron gate with the phrase *Arbeit Macht Frei*. Though used as a prison work camp, it contained a small underground gas chamber. Birkenau, the much larger camp, had row upon row of one-story wooden barracks and was entered through the long brick building with the watchtower over the central arch through which the trains came with their human cargo—so often photographed it has become an icon for the camp, itself a monument to those who suffered there. It is the Birkenau camp that contained the large gas chambers and crematoria.

it is known, this "liberation" was the only achievement of that type during the entire German occupation.

Near the end of the war, Schindler transferred his Kraków factory, together with the Jews who worked it, to Czechoslovakia. It was there that they were liberated. The day before the official liberation, however, they disarmed the German guards without a struggle and became free people. There were about 1,200 of them, and today they live on all continents—the Schindler Jews.

Leopold "Poldek" Page settled with his wife in Los Angeles. Until recently he had a leather-goods store in Beverly Hills, but now he only operates in the wholesale side of the business. One day in 1980 a well-known Australian writer, Thomas Keneally, came to the store. He wanted to buy a new briefcase. Poldek likes to get to know people and does so very easily, so he asked his customer who he was.

"A writer."

"A good one?" asked Poldek.

"Some think so—in any case I make a living out of it," answered Keneally.

"Then I have a story for you for the theme of a book," said Poldek.

Hearing such a declaration, a writer tries to escape, because every day a few people want to tell him a "completely unusual story," but when Keneally finished listening to Poldek's story, he said, "I'll write this book." It was ready in two years and published by a major New York house—Simon and Schuster. Subsequently it has received numerous prizes and has been published all over the world.

I read about the book for the first time in the book review section of *Newsweek*, at the beginning of 1983.* In the fall of 1984, I was to go to the United States of America on a grant from the U.S. Information Agency, and I discussed my plans for the trip with friends. One of them, Jan Krejcza, told me that

---

*January 10, 1983, v. 101, p. 64.

if I got to Los Angeles I should bring greetings to his old school friend. "We were brought up when we were kids on Kalwaryjska Street. He is a wonderful man, a Polish Jew. He is devoted to Kraków and Poland. He was saved from the Holocaust thanks to a German, Oskar Schindler." It dawned on me that I had already heard something about this—the brief review in *Newsweek*. Jan Krejcza gave me the address of Leopold Page, a.k.a. Poldek. Later, in Washington, D.C., when the organizers of my tour asked what I dreamed to do (yes, literally!), I answered that I would like to meet Poldek. Thanks to an AT&T operator finding a Los Angeles telephone number in less than a minute, I soon made contact with Poldek. Enthused by my call, he invited me to visit him.

Ten days later I found myself in Los Angeles. Minutes after I moved into my room at the Hilton, the phone rang. It was Poldek.

"I'll come for you right away," said Poldek. "Come to the main entrance."

I had doubts. "How will I recognize you?"

"Nothing simpler," answered Poldek, "you will see a 'typical Jew.'"

"What do you mean by a 'typical Jew'?"

"Well, I have blue eyes...."

As additional identification, Poldek added that he would sit in a Cadillac and that he was "seventy years young." Since then, that's how I always think of him; though in March 1993 Poldek turned eighty, so to me he is eighty years young.

We spent several hours in the back of his store, in the same place where months earlier he had convinced Thomas Keneally to write *Schindler's List*. At the end of our meeting he said, "You'll see. Some day Steven Spielberg will make a film based on this book."

"Poldek, it seems to me it is impossible. Steven Spielberg does not make such films. This is a wonderful story, yes, but it is not *E.T.* or *Close Encounters*." By then we were already such good friends that I could say this to him, and, of course, this was before *The Color Purple* (1985), which broke from the pattern of Spielberg's previous work. In 1984, though, when one talked about Spielberg one thought of a creator of adventure films or science fiction.

Poldek would not change his mind and repeated the same thing every time we saw each other. A year after our first meeting he came to Kraków with his wife, Mila. I made a twenty-minute film about him for Polish television. Then, two years later, I did several interviews with Poldek and Mila on the topic of *Schindler's List* for the Kraków TV station's news magazine. (After one of these I received an ugly anonymous letter.) Though Keneally's *Schindler's List* was translated into Polish, Wydawnictwo Literackie, the Polish publishing company in Kraków, did not consider it a good investment.* Around the rest of the world, it already was receiving mixed reactions. Early in our friendship, I once asked Poldek about its acceptance in Los Angeles. I did not want official reviews, those I knew were excellent; I wanted to know what his Jewish friends thought. He became sadly pensive for a moment, though he is a man full of optimism—a quality which he thinks helped him to survive the war.

"In the Talmud† there is a saying which appears on the medal for the 'Righteous'‡: 'Whoever saves one life, saves the world entire.' Thus Schindler saved the world twelve hundred times."

---

*The Polish edition of *Schindler's List* was published by a Warsaw publishing house in 1993, a few months after this book was published.

†The Talmud contains two written commentaries on Jewish law, one from Palestine (ca. A.D. 375) and one from Babylonia (ca. A.D. 500).

‡The medal for the "Righteous Among the Nations" is awarded by Yad Vashem, the Holocaust Martyrs and Heroes Remembrance Authority in Jerusalem. Yad Vashem is a memorial archive, museum, and research and education center dedicated to documenting the Holocaust. An important aspect of its mission is to identify and honor the "Righteous Ones" whose efforts resulted in saving many Jewish lives, and by doing so, saving the future generations of many families.

"It is a beautiful statement, beautifully said," I answered, "but there are some who say that he simply made a lot of money on these twelve hundred Jews."

"Yes, I know those arguments," agreed Poldek, "but what is the price of life?"

"There is no price," I answered with certainty. But I asked him to stop avoiding the issue of my statement.

"Yes," said Poldek, "you can say that he was buying our lives, but he did not make any money on us. After the war, an independent commission figured out that he spent four million marks, or roughly one million dollars, on feeding his Jews."

"Where did he get it?" I asked, because the number seemed astronomical.

"Do you know the value of so simple an object as an enamel pot during the war?" Poldek answered with a question and continued: "Sometimes more than a gold ring. Schindler sold a part of his products on the black market and with that money he bought gold and jewelry. He always paid for them honestly and kept nothing for himself, using the 'treasures' for bribes. When I found him several years after the war, he was a destitute, lonely, sick man without means of support. We helped him then, sending him money each month from the people he saved. When he died, already decorated with a medal for the 'Righteous Among the Nations' from Yad Vashem* in Israel, he was buried in Jerusalem, as he had wished."

Though I heard categorical assurance in his every word, I had to ask Poldek one more question—about something I heard somewhere, I don't remember where. "Is it true that within the Jewish community people were offended that you initiated a book praising a German in the context of the Holocaust?"

"Yes." Poldek's voice was full of sorrow. "Some stopped speaking to me.... You know, there were some whom I had

---

*Yad Vashem honored Oskar Schindler with a medal and the planting of a tree in May 1961, thirteen years before his death on October 9, 1974.

considered to be my friends for years. Too bad. I feel it is my duty to praise a noble man. According to the Jewish Chassidim* there are never more than thirty-six in the whole world. I would like to live long enough to see Steven Spielberg, who bought the rights to film the book for four hundred thousand dollars, make the film in my dear Kraków."

Since then, every time Poldek asked me when *Schindler's List* would be published in Poland, I answered in turn with a question: "When will Steven Spielberg make a film in Kraków?" I believed it would happen, when that Sunday morning Poldek said, "Dear,"—Poldek calls everybody "dear"—"Spielberg flies in to Kraków the day after tomorrow and I want you to meet and accompany him."

The next day Janek Janik, an executive with Heritage Films, the newly privatized Polish film studio, called me with the same proposal. He was very secretive. When he found out that I knew all about Schindler, he said, "You know, somebody very important is arriving."

I interrupted, "Yes, yes, I know who is arriving who is so important."

"How do you know? This is a big secret."

I reassured Janik that it was all right. I knew from Poldek Page.

A day later the head of Heritage Films himself, Lew Rywin, showed up in Kraków. Though I have worked twenty years in Polish television, this was my first encounter with the longtime

---

*The Chassidim are a Jewish sect from the second century B.C. that believed in strict adherence to ritual law and generally rejected the Hellenistic trends of the eastern Mediterranean. Around 1750 a Jewish mystical sect taking the same name was founded in Poland. The sect was also fundamentalist in that it rejected the rationalism that characterized eighteenth-century European enlightenment and emphasized the strict observance of ritual.

executive of Poltel—the technical wing of Polish Television, Poland's equivalent to BBC-TV. In 1989, after the political changes in Poland, Andrzej Drawicz became the president of Polish Television and made Lew Rywin his deputy. When Drawicz left for an academic career, Lew Rywin resigned from television and formed his own studio, Heritage Films, which already had credits from Agnieszka Holland's *Europa, Europa*. Now there was the prospect of coproducing a film with Steven Spielberg.

Steven Spielberg's arrival was impossible to keep secret. The day before, a Paris correspondent spread the news. At Balice Airport a group of Kraków newsmen was already waiting. We greeted Spielberg at the steps of the airplane. He conveyed greetings from Poldek and agreed to make a brief statement for the press under the condition that afterwards they would not keep stalking him. Then, holding a small 8mm video camera, he walked over to the Kraków television crew and said that here he intended to make the truest of all his films. He had come to personally and most intimately experience the places where the story of the Schindler Jews played out. Coproducer Jerry Molen, scriptwriter Steven Zaillian, and a secretary, Bonnie Curtis, accompanied him. From Heritage Films, in addition to Lew Rywin, there were Kasia Trocka—Lew's right-hand assistant, Jan Janik, and Marek Brodzki, a young director. I also found myself in that small group.

"On to Birkenau!" ordered Lew Rywin.

The concentration camp in Birkenau takes up very little space in the book or the screenplay, but it is important to the Schindler story because in the fall of 1944 three hundred women from Schindler's factory in Kraków were supposed to travel to a new Schindler factory in Brinnlitz. Instead, their train of cattle wagons mistakenly took them to Birkenau, where they were imprisoned for several weeks. Schindler negotiated with the authorities and retrieved "his" Jewish women. At the point when they were on the train again, happy that they were leaving hell, another train pulled onto the adjoining track. The fragment of the screenplay reads:

> When the wagons with the women are being closed, the doors of the adjoining train open and people begin to pour out. Through the uproar one can hear a scream from the locked wagon. One of the Schindler's women recognizes her young son among those leaving the train.

This is an authentic event. The woman was Regina Horowitz, the child, Ryszard Horowitz. Originally from Kraków, he now lives in New York City and is internationally recognized as one of the country's best commercial photographers. Some time ago, as I was tracing the lives of Schindler Jews, I wrote an article for the Polish magazine *Przekrój* about meeting with him in his New York studio. Ryszard Horowitz remained in Birkenau until the liberation—January 1945.

Birkenau is deserted in the middle of January. Cold, windy. Spielberg pulls his parka hood over his head. Almost continuously he holds a small 8mm video camera to his eye documenting his mission in Poland. We climb up to the former watchtower over the main gate. From here there is a chilling view of rows of stumps of broken chimneys from the burned up barracks. Later we cross the railway tracks on which the transports arrived, and through a barbed wire fence we walk into one of the still-preserved women's barracks. There are the original wooden board "beds"—just like lumber storage racks. Spielberg is asking for details on life in the camp: How many prisoners to one bed? How was the selection on the ramp conducted?

We are standing at a small wooden barrack where the matter of life or death was decided. Being sent left or right meant life. Being sent forward meant going directly to the gas chambers. Their ruins are now covered with snow. Spielberg moves away from us toward those ruins, stops, and stands motionless for a moment as if meditating—there will be many more such moments.

He puts down the camera for the first time. It is as though he wants to absorb the impressions with all his senses. Quietly he looks at Birkenau's winter landscape, listening to the eerie whine of the wind through the barbed wires; he wants to experience the penetrating chill of January in Birkenau camp.

Then, in quiet, simple meditation he stands motionless for a time at the monument where a while ago he placed a bouquet of roses.

"I do not feel any sorrow; I feel anger," he tells us.

Next stop: a very short visit to Auschwitz, the main camp. We are walking from the gate with the inscription *Arbeit Macht Frei* [Work Makes One Free] to the gallows on which Rudolf Hoess, the commander of the camp, was executed. We stop for a while in the small subterranean gas chamber and crematorium. Spielberg is especially moved, seeing a deeply worn wooden threshold quietly testifying to the passage of thousands—a symbol for those other thresholds crossed by millions. Here this single threshold to just a small gassing facility is worn through almost to the ground by victims who did not know what awaited them on the other side. As Steven leaves the crematorium he rests his hand on the wooden door frame at the place where in the Jewish home a mezuzah* hangs. It is touched each time as one enters or exits a home. He holds his hand on the door frame for a long time, as if he wanted to feel a common bond with those who could never leave from there.

Returning to Kraków, we want to take a look at the Liban

---

*The mezuzah consists of a parchment containing two specific passages from Deuteronomy on one side and the name of God on the other. It is folded and placed in a case, often decorated with the emblem of the Ark of the Covenant, mounted on left side of the door frame so that the name of God is visible from the outside as one enters the home. This is done in accordance with the commands found in the biblical passages quoted on the parchment: Deut. 6:4–9; 11:13–21.

quarry. The place has nothing to do with the Płaszów camp
from where the Schindler Jews were "recruited," but it is a
lifelike setting for the film. Next to the walls stand old rusty
mills once used to grind chalk stones. Higher up there is a road
to the ramp and old pumps. Nothing would have to be changed
if scenes of work in the camp were to be filmed here. The
silence in the old quarry is frightening. From somewhere up
above in the stillness comes the cry of a pheasant.

We leave Liban and ride to the site of the former camp in
Płaszów, turning onto Jerozolimska Street. Fresh snow makes a
smooth cover over the former camp where, according to historians' estimates, some forty to eighty thousand people perished
within its approximately 173 acres. Not far from the place
where there are still fragments of a former Jewish cemetery, a
flock of thrushes feeds on hawthorn berries. The road is
slippery and full of potholes; we drive slowly up the hill to the
monument. From here one has a good view of the area of the
former camp. Even through the fog one can see some of the new
buildings of Płaszów. The gray house where the administration
of the camp was situated stands against the background of an
apartment high-rise that a few months ago was not there. It is a
pity, because any shots from that place are out of the question.
Spielberg notes that fact on the camera, which he treats as if it
were a pocket notebook.

The wind is cold and penetrating as we walk to the monument. I tell Spielberg about an old Austrian fort here where,
during the war, they executed many prisoners from the Płaszów
camp as well as from Kraków prisons such as Montelupich and
St. Michael, among others. When I was here filming a report
about Poldek, I found out that the prisoners had an obscene
name for the place—Chujowa Górka [Prick Hill]. If one was
brought here, one was as good as dead. Poldek and I found
several carbine shells and bullets right on the edge of the road. I
showed Spielberg one of these—Poldek took the others to the
Holocaust Museum in Los Angeles. Spielberg silently films the
shell in the palm of my hand.

There is another place in Podgórze important for Spielberg to see: Wzgórze Lasoty [Lasota Hill] on which Oskar Schindler had an experience that touched his soul and made him decide to save as many Jews as possible. According to Keneally's book, when Schindler went horseback riding with his girlfriend, he was standing on the edge of the hill from where he watched the liquidation of the ghetto. He saw a little girl of about four years old in a red dress—he would not forget.

Spielberg wants to see the very spot where the event took place because it is planned to be one of the most important scenes in the film. We drive up to the Austrian fort of St. Benedict, then we wade on foot through the deep snow and stop on the edge of the hill, not far from the small church of St. Benedict. We can see a small segment of Rękawka Street, which once was a border of the Kraków ghetto. Most of the view is obscured by the trees and bushes which have been growing for the last fifty years. We try a different place, somewhat lower. It is better—one can see a little more. It would be enough to cut a bit off the tops of the bushes. Spielberg will possibly want to film that scene from this vantage point, because he is recording each detail, every possible setting.

The path we are taking leads us lower and lower onto Rękawka Street. It is very slippery. Children are using it as a snow slide; some slide on sleds and some on plastic bags. There is a broken sled leaning against a tree. Spielberg takes videos of children sliding down.

"Michał!" One can hear a call from across the street. "Come home!"

"Yeah, right away!" a boy answers from the hilltop. "Only one more time, one more glide down!"

Michał will return home in a moment, and after dinner he will watch TV. It is possible he will look at one of Spielberg's films, but he does not know that a while ago he himself was acting in a film by Steven Spielberg.

The cars pull up on the street below. There is a school a few steps away from here. In the back of it is one of two remaining fragments of the Kraków ghetto wall, which connects the corner of the school building to the rock formations on Krzemionki Hill. In one place the wall is low enough that one can get a glimpse inside the former ghetto. This spot is made for the film. Maybe it will be used.

We visit the ghetto museum, located in the former Apteka Pod Orłem [Pharmacy under the Eagle]. We look at the photographs and documents from the time of the war,* then walk down Jósefińska Street. We pass a bank—during the war it was occupied by the *Judenrat* [the Jewish self-rule committee required of the Jewish community by the German occupation authorities]. Here Poldek came to have the coveted blue stamp placed on his yellow *Kennkarta* [identification card], which would permit him to remain in the ghetto and thus save him from being sent to the concentration camp. Only skilled laborers were eligible for this privilege.

"Occupation?" asked an official of the *Judenrat*.

"Teacher."

"That's not an occupation."

"Well, put down locksmith." Poldek once worked in his uncle's small shop.

"Ah...that's an occupation."

Poldek received the precious stamp.

Poldek lived a short distance from here, at 2 Jósefińska Street. I lead Spielberg there. On a wall in the courtyard is an old tablet inscribed in Hebrew. Some of the walls have holes in them large enough so that one can pass from one yard to another. It was covert openings such as these that Poldek took to pass to the Aryan side—through cellars, holes, and little-known passageways. On the other side he would take off the white armband with the Star of David and go to meet Schindler. A year ago, during Page's visit, we ate ripe cherries from the trees growing in the courtyard. Now, Spielberg delights in eating pickles which Lew Rywin found at a neighborhood stand. We enter the

---

*Typically in this text, "the war" will refer to World War II.

courtyard of the next house. Here, too, it is as if time had stopped fifty years ago—wooden gangways and balconies typical of Kazimierz* and Podgórze. In the courtyard there is an old locksmith shop. Is that where Poldek worked? We lead Spielberg to the bank of the Wisła (Vistula) River so that he may look at the bridge over which the Jews trudged when they were "resettled" from their homes in Kraków and Kazimierz to the ghetto. There is a cold wind along the river from the west. Swans float on the water.

It is still light—three o'clock in the afternoon. We decide to take a ride to the center of Kraków, which Spielberg has not yet seen. We drive to Floriańska Street. Spielberg admires the Floriańska Gate. We proceed to the cafe Jama Michalika [Michael's Cave], a stylish period place which could be used for some of the scenes in the film. He likes it. A quarter of an hour later we enter the interior of the Marjacki Bazylika [St. Mary's Basilica], with its extraordinary late-medieval high altar triptych sculptured by Wit Stwosz [Veit Stoss], an artist from Nuremberg. The screenplay calls for that location.

Spielberg has been on his feet for many hours. Time for some rest. When we approach the front door of the Grand Hotel, Spielberg, holding the camera in filming position, gives Bonnie an order: "Stop." She freezes. Another order: "Action." We open the door to start in, when all burst out laughing. Spielberg had given his first directorial instructions in Kraków.

The next day's schedule is intense: in the morning a visit to the prison on Pomorska Street. I translate for Spielberg the inscriptions scratched by prisoners on the walls of the cells in the basement of this former Gestapo headquarters. Then a walk

---

*Kazimierz is a Kraków district named for King Kazimierz the Great, who was responsibile for bringing Jews to Kraków in the fourteenth century. He envisioned their being of great help in establishing Kraków as a center of finance and commerce. Before the war most Jews lived in this district. The great Old Synagogue is there on Szeroka Street, as are several historic sites. The Ariel Cafe, which became Steven Spielberg's favorite evening cabaret cafe, is also here.

through the corridors of the building where Schindler spent a few days—rather comfortably, though under suspicion. Next on the schedule—the prison on Montelupich. Here, too, Schindler spent time when he was reported to the Gestapo. He was able to get out of here also, thanks to timely bribes—after all, one does not kill a goose that lays golden eggs. I must admit to being ill at ease for a few moments—nervous when they took all our documents at the gate and we were told to wait in the hallway of Montelupich Prison for the warden. I joked with Janek Janik, asking if he arranged for *both* passes—one in and one out. As it turned out, the warden was a colleague from the university, so we all had a good laugh.

Spielberg looks at the hallways, peeks into the prison barber shop. Then he wants to see a standard cell, which could have housed Schindler. The "tenants" of such a cell were temporarily transferred so that the film director could inspect the locale. We take a look into a small prison cell. Spielberg inspects everything through the viewfinder of his camera. Noting the modern TV on the wall, Lew Rywin comments, "Steven, you can be sure they did not have a color TV set when Schindler was here." As the warden takes us to the courtyard, he says that Amon Goeth, the commander of the Płaszów concentration camp, was a prisoner here while he awaited sentencing. All the prisoners are waving arms from the barred windows. Somehow it had become known through the prisoners' secret communication system that Spielberg was a visitor.

Next stop is the main building of AGH [the Academy of Mining and Smelting]. During the war, this was the site of the German occupation government for the "General Gubernia"— or Poland, as it was no longer allowed to be called. The architecture of the building fascinates Spielberg. He would like to use it in his film but it is not certain that it can be worked into the school's teaching schedule. After that, a glimpse of the house where Schindler lived. Later a trip to Kazimierz. Mr. Jakubowicz, head of the Jewish community in Kraków, is our guide through the old Remuh Cemetery and the Old Synagogue. There Spielberg says,

"I wish my parents could see this."

"Are they from this part of Europe?" I ask.

"Yes, from Austria, somewhere."

Later we propose that Steven visit a butcher shop in the round building on Plac Nowy [New Square], usually called the Jewish Square. It had been featured in several films. One of the butchers sharpens his knife and says to Spielberg, "Hi! Last night I saw you on TV when you arrived in your private jet."

Time to visit an especially important place: Schindler's enamel factory on Lipowa Street. At present it is occupied by a segment of Telpod, Inc., but the old architecture from the warremains. The gate that had separated the Schindler subcamp from the rest of the world is still the same. Spielberg is obviously pleased seeing the authentic environment. Knowing that Telpod has economic problems, I propose that Spielberg buy the factory instead of renting it. He could be a full-fledged proprietor like Schindler, I add. Everybody is amused by the proposal, but it's obvious that Spielberg does not want to trade being a film director and producer for the privilege of becoming a producer of electronic parts.

We are in a hurry to meet Andrzej Wajda,** who is to join us for lunch at the Grand Hotel. One by one my collection of photos of Oskar Schindler is passed around. Wajda talks about the insights he gained while making his films about World War

*Andrzej Wajda is among Poland's greatest and certainly most famous film and stage directors. His films include *Kanal* (1956), *Ashes and Diamonds* (1958), and *Korczak* (1990). His films *Man of Marble* (1976) and *Man of Iron* (1981) are internationally recognized for their remarkably open and candid portrayal of Lech Walesa's struggle as he led the strikes and protests that resulted in the founding of Solidarity. This daring Polish labor movement is credited with initiating the process by which Poland moved toward a return to democracy and the nation it is today.

II, and about his personal experiences during the war. Spielberg listens intently. This short personal meeting between the two great directors surely enriched Spielberg's imagination and knowledge of wartime Poland. Listening to this informal chat between Steven Spielberg and Andrzej Wajda, I had to pinch myself every so often to be sure I was not dreaming.

Spielberg tells us about his meeting with President Ronald Reagan in the White House, where they watched *E.T.* After the showing, the president, a former actor himself, had only one criticism: "The final list of credits is definitely too long." Spielberg's comment was, "We like honoring everyone contributing to a film's production to such an extent that sometimes the credits alone may be five minutes long." I am thinking, Many must already be dreaming of finding their names among the credits for *Schindler's List*.

At the end of our visit I offer Spielberg the shell which I showed him in Płaszów. "I will keep it as a cherished keepsake," says Steven, and he carefully puts it away, along with a piece of barbed wire from the fence around the crematorium ruins in Birkenau. I ask him to write something in my copy of *Schindler's List*, which Poldek had given me years ago. He writes, "For Frank. I hope this will make your dreams come true. Steven Spielberg."

Just before the departure to the airport where the engines of Spielberg's plane had been warming up, I ask Steve Zaillian, the scriptwriter, to evaluate the visit to Kraków. "It seems," he answers, "that it is more of a spiritual experience. Spielberg did not have to come to Kraków in order to see how to make *Schindler's List*—that he knows perfectly well. He came here to reassure himself that he must make this film."

2

This Will Be a Film About a Good German and About a Bad German

Steven Spielberg spent thirty-six hours in Kraków. Saying goodbye and getting into his private jet, which would take him to London, he told Lew Rywin, "I want you to build me a replica of the Płaszów Camp for *Schindler's List*—but not on the original site."

A few weeks later the first members of the production staff for *Schindler's List* arrived in Kraków. Among them was Allan Starski, the production designer, who was to design 146 settings required at the thirty-five locations. He had designed *Europa, Europa* (Germany, Poland, 1990) for Agnieszka Holland, *Paper Marriage* (Poland, 1992) for Krzysztof Lang, and *Korczak* (Poland, 1990) for Andrzej Wajda. His television credits include Jack Gold's *Escape From Sobibor* (Yugoslavia, 1987). It would appear that a better choice of designer could not have been made. Wajda's serial took place in Kraków at the end of the nineteenth and the beginning of the twentieth century, so Allan Starski was already very familiar with the city and its environs. In addition, his achievement in designing concentration camp sets earned him an Emmy nomination for *Escape From Sobibor*. To produce a replica of Płaszów camp, however, would be a greater task: It could become the largest single design project so far in the history of Polish film. Moreover, if one were to rank it among cinematic replicas of concentration or prison camps—who knows—it may have become the largest in the history of world cinema.

A search begins for open spaces and buildings in Kraków and vicinity. There is need for old factory exteriors, interior spaces with old machinery in working condition, and various other settings associated with factory operations. Also, a site for reconstructing the camp must be found.

We are looking for suitable sites with Ewa Braun, a set decorator and design collaborator with Allan Starski. We visit quarries near Krzeszowice, wonderful sites, but they have two disadvantages: They are working quarries, so a payment for a pause in production during construction and filming would put a burden on the budget. The other inconvenience is their twenty-mile distance. Daily trips for the crew and hundreds of extras would take additional time, and winter days are short. Filming could take place only between 9 A.M. and 2 P.M., which would mean extending the shooting schedule. In short—cost is an important factor.

From my spring and summer excursions into Kraków environs I remember a place which, thanks to the character of its terrain, almost faithfully replicates the place where the Płaszów camp was built. Furthermore, it is near Kraków and is administered by the city. An undeveloped open space in Pychowice Valley leaning towards the Wisła River, it is a favorite place for training novice aviators. On top of the hill there are fragments of an old Austrian fort, just as on Chujowa Górka, in Płaszów. Nearby is only an old brick factory, and no modern buildings are visible to spoil the image in a camera viewfinder. On the horizon, past the Wisła River, is the Bielany region; against the sky one can see the Kameduły Monastery. We drive to the valley. Ewa Braun, with Grażna Kozłowska, an assistant to Micheł Szczerbic, the production manager, takes photographs in all directions. She likes the place but she finds one fault—there is only one road to the top of the hill. Several roads must be built to accommodate trucks with building materials for constructing the camp barracks, fencing, and the like. This is a big obstacle, but the final decision is Spielberg's. If he likes the place, the roads will be built.

In mid-June Spielberg returned to Kraków. This meant he had decided to film *Schindler's List* here and not in Czechoslovakia, something that had been a possibility early on. This visit would have a different character. The previous one was sort of a historical pilgrimage to contact the authentic places linked to Oskar Schindler, something in the way of a "tryout" of on-the-spot history for a man who was visiting central Europe for the first time. This director, who had made one film with an historical background, *The Color Purple* (1985), but who really made films to entertain mass audiences, suddenly realized that now he must create something completely different.

The second visit was a typical business trip. Spielberg wanted to see the fifty-some sites that Heritage Films had proposed. The schedule in Poland was very tight. Less than an hour was available to inspect each site, including traveling time—an insane schedule. As it happened, I was engaged in organizing a European Month of Culture for the Office of the Press and so could not accompany Spielberg's crew uninterruptedly, as I had done the previous January. I could not deny myself, however, the pleasure of meeting Spielberg at the Kraków airport. This time the Polish film contingent was larger. Lew Rywin was joined by Allan Starski, Ewa Braun, and Micheł Szczerbic, one could say, the Polish leaders in the field. Spielberg was accompanied by Bonnie Curtis and coproducers Jerry Molen and

Branko Lustig. *Schindler's List* would be the fourth film Jerry Molen produced for Spielberg; the others were *The Color Purple* (1985), *Hook* (1991), and *Jurassic Park* (1993). Additional films to Jerry's credit include *Tootsie* (1982), *Rain Man* (1988), *Days of Thunder* (1990), *Bright Lights, Big City* (1988), **batteries not included* (1987), *A Soldier's Story* (1984), *The Postman Always Rings Twice* (1981), and *Ordinary People* (1980).

Dressed in his customary jeans and getting into a minibus which will transport him around Kraków and vicinity, Steven Spielberg turned to me and said, "You know, my film turned out perfectly." For a moment I do not understand which film he is talking about. Everybody knows that in his twenty-some years of work he has had at least twenty years of success. From a financial point of view alone, his films have grossed the highest in the history of filmmaking. On the official list of the "All-Time Top Fifty Movies" about half are films directed by or produced by Spielberg. In 1991, *E.T. The Extra-Terrestrial* (1982) was in first place, with $228,618,939 and the seventh, eighth, ninth, and tenth were *Jaws* (1975) and the *Indiana Jones Trilogy* (1981, 1984, 1989), which collectively brought in close to $500 million. So, at first, I did not understand what film Steven was talking about. After a moment, though, everything was clear. He was talking about the videos he took on his first visit to Kraków. These were really his personal creation. Once before, he told me that the only films he considered his personal creations were those like the one he made of his little daughter in front of a TV set—like all those taken by a proud and loving father. His other films are all the result of teamwork—by the director, scriptwriter, production designer, camera crews, and even the people in advertising and promotion. He believes such cooperative work is the basis of the success or failure of any professional film.

Not far from the Hotel Forum, where Spielberg was staying this time, there is an old tannery building. Spielberg wanted to see it. In the large abandoned rooms there are some old hydraulic presses, other machinery, and kettles. This could be a place for building Schindler's factory in Brinnlitz (Czechoslovakia). As we were walking out Steven ran upstairs, curious about what was there. "Here we could have a space for lodging the Schindler workers," he said. All the time he looked, observed, and thought in terms of different scenes from the script. It occurred to me that it would be really convenient—and would save him time and money. The crew could be housed at the Hotel Forum and a two-minute walk would bring them onto the set for filming.

That evening the dean of Polish cinematography, Waldemar Dąbrowski joined us for dinner at Wierzynek, one of the most famous and elegant places for Polish dishes in Kraków. After dinner Lew talked Spielberg into going to Piwnica Pod Baranami [The Cellar under the Rams], a well-known cabaret and nightclub featuring music and satiric skits. Spielberg had heard of it—from Zbigniew Preissner, with whom he had had dinner in Hollywood. "OK, I'll go, but only for fifteen minutes," warned Spielberg, and he stayed for three hours—until the end of the performance. Thanks to that, Jacek Wójcicki and Beata Rybotycka, both famous cabaret artists and regulars at "the Cellar," had time to arrive. They were a few miles out of town at the television studios in Łęg taking part in a concert dedicated to the playwright Witkacy—part of the "European Month of Culture" I had organized. So Steven was able to enjoy their best songs and cabaret numbers. "I would like them in my film," Spielberg said to Lew Rywin, who was sitting next to him translating some of their hilarious jokes. I was translating too—for Jerry Molen, so he did not sit in the Cellar listening to what for someone not knowing Polish must have sounded like alien gibberish. All our guests enjoyed themselves, though, as Jerry admitted, he was dying of exhaustion after two days of intensive location documentation.*

---

*In the motion picture industry, documenting a location is the process of recording via photos, videos, sketches, descriptive notes, etc., the details of a specific site that might be utilized in the production.

Next morning, at 8:00 A.M. as we drove to the airport, I asked if the present visit will cause changes in the script. "Oh, yes, a lot!" Spielberg answered. I gave him a copy of *Przekrój* magazine containing my article on his first visit to Kraków and we had time to take souvenir photos in front of the airplane. Then we said, "Goodbye till next time." That "next time" would be the following February, on the set of *Schindler's List*.

When I asked Lew Rywin for his impressions of the second visit to Kraków, he quoted what Spielberg said on the way to the airport: "If I could, I would start the production of *Schindler's List* immediately, but I have another job to finish—filming *Jurassic Park* in Hawaii."

After that film was finished Spielberg would come back to Kraków, where he had already chosen most of the locations. Many scenes would be filmed in Kazimierz, the old Jewish district. There also, on Szeroka Street, scenes would be filmed which actually took place on Plac Zgody, the square in the former ghetto. The Płaszów camp would be reconstructed in the Liban quarry. Fragments of buildings marked for demolition that belong to Solvay, a former chemical company, would also be used, as would the Bonarka train station, an enamelware factory in Olkusz, and a military base near Skarżyska Kamiennej.

Rywin told me of an amusing incident that happened during the location documentation process. As they were entering a hall in the enamel factory at Olkusz a guard stopped them.

"No entry! Restricted!"

Well, if you can't, you can't. It seemed to be a big secret that they were manufacturing pots for the army. On the other hand, at the military installation near Skarżyska, where there could be a reason to suspect the capitalistic war mongers (as they called westerners not long ago), to the question of whether an American director could, if it was necessary…eventually… the answer was: "A film made here by an American director? But of course, with pleasure! Tomorrow!" Three years ago it would have been impossible. Well—times were changing.

I wanted to look at a hall in the Kraków military depot chiefly engaged in refurbishing equipment to see if it would be suitable for the film. When they finally decided to let me in, after much discussion and reconfirmation of my benign intent—"No photographs, please!"—I discovered they were only refurbishing some old military trucks.

As the head of Heritage Films, Lew Rywin did not want his part in the Spielberg film production to be merely facilitating a Hollywood effort, as the Yugoslavs and Spaniards had been doing for Americans in years past. He wanted to convince Polish business to invest Polish money in the enterprise; that way Poland could feel like a joint partner in the success that the film surely would have. At the same time he had many qualms. His main fear was the greed that might be exhibited by people with whom he would have to cooperate. Many would think that in return for working with Spielberg one could ask for the sky, but *Schindler's List* was not the usual super-production for which Universal Pictures typically would pour out large sums of money.

We know from experience, said Lew Rywin, that Holocaust films are not money makers. Universal Pictures agreed to Spielberg's choice under the condition that it would be a low-budget production. All the partners had to be prepared to be reasonable. Despite these concerns, Rywin concluded it would be an important experience. For many, the work on this film would be comparable to obtaining a doctorate in filmmaking and, in the case of set designer Allan Starski, rather like getting nominated to a professorship.

Jerry Molen had similar concerns. He stayed behind in Kraków for several hours, so I had the opportunity to talk with him after saying goodbye to Spielberg. "We are facing the most difficult task," he said, "setting the budget and convincing the decision-makers at Universal that they should invest money in the production of *Schindler's List*. If we win this round of the production process, nothing will stand in our way to begin building a replica of the Płaszów camp in three or four months. This is the most important construction project in the film production—and the most costly."

Many trips were made between Warsaw and Los Angeles. Allan Starski took his design proposals for Spielberg's approval. Videocassettes brought images of sites which Spielberg had not seen during his two visits. Other videos presented Polish actors that Heritage Films wanted to cast in *Schindler's List*.

In Kraków there were casting calls for extras—at least 2,500 were needed. Various objects, including costume pieces, original documents, and books of the period were collected. At least 1,000 suitcases of the period were needed. There was an unsuccessful search to find a period checkbook from the war for Oskar Schindler. A space for the production office was found. Finally, Steven Spielberg and his family needed a house for three months. At last Donna Smith arrived—a senior vice president in charge of production for Universal Pictures. Her senior ranking came because of her position in the company's corporate structure. She supervises the production of some fifty films at any given time.

I am supposed to meet Donna Smith in the Hotel Forum. She has already inspected villas in the Kraków suburb of Wola Justowska, where Spielberg's family could be residing. They need several bedrooms and bathrooms for five children and their nannies. "It was a difficult task but not impossible to accomplish," she says when I ask about the outcome of the search. Just two days earlier she signed an agreement between Universal Pictures and Heritage Films for coproduction. The Polish newspaper *Gazeta Wyborcza** reported the event, and also

---

**Gazeta Wyborcza* is the biggest Polish daily newspaper. It was

a humorous exchange between Donna and Branko Lustig pertaining to the meaning of the term *low-budget film*. The difference between their perspectives as American and central European producers amounted to only a paltry $50 million. What other information did I obtain about Donna? Her fore-fathers came from Moravia, but it was the senior vice president's first visit to Kraków, or, for that matter, central Europe.

We are sitting in the coffee shop of the Hotel Forum admiring the sunset. After two rainy days there is a play of colors on the sky framing the old Kameduły Monastery on Bielany Hill. Donna agrees that the sunset here is as beautiful as those portrayed in Hollywood movies. She encountered the Oskar Schindler story about two years ago, after the script was already written. Spielberg seemed to be interested in the topic to fulfill the desire to come closer to his Jewish roots. I inquire about the implications of the coproduction agreement. She explains that until now Universal Pictures had not worked with producers in Poland, and it is certain that all American film companies will be watching this production with great interest, for it may influence future cooperative endeavors.

Though realizing that it is not polite to talk about money matters, I casually mention my understanding that the amount of the film's budget has not been resolved. Donna confirms. From other sources I had found out that this is not the lowest budget in Steven's career. *The Color Purple* (1985) was his least expensive film. The total cost was only $15 million, but it received eleven Oscar nominations. The truth is, it is not just a matter of money.

"Does the company think that the film will be profitable?" I ask. "I was told that the topic of the Holocaust does not sell well. Some feel it would be better if Spielberg just made a donation to the Holocaust Museum rather than make the film."

Donna Smith simply answers that when one works in the film

---

established by members of Solidarity before the first free postwar elections were held in 1989.

business and spends millions of dollars, one thinks of profits, not losses. "Of course, in this case, at Universal one does not just consider money. They know it is not going to be *E.T.* or *Indiana Jones*, but something different. If we thought about this film just in terms of a business," Donna continues, "maybe we would produce it somewhere else and probably cheaper, but we recognize that Poland and Kraków are the only places where *Schindler's List* can and should be made."

Branko Lustig, one of the producers for *Schindler's List*, has been in the film business for forty years. His credits include *Fiddler on the Roof* (1971), *The Tin Drum* (1979), *Sophie's Choice* (1982), and *The Winds of War* (1983). If one wanted to meet him it was easiest at 6:00 A.M. when he started his daily jogging. He did not change his routine, even in Kraków. He started from the Hotel Forum on the boulevard along the Wisła River to the Podgórze Bridge—the same one which was to be used in the film. He crossed the bridge and jogged toward Wawel Castle.

When I first met Branko he was dressed in his jeans and running shoes. He came to Kraków to prepare for Spielberg's second visit to study sites for the film. Together with Heritage Films executive Janek Janik, he traveled to all the places proposed for sets by the Polish coproducers. He also wanted to visit the president* of the city in order to obtain a declaration of cooperation with the filming crew from the city officials, but, sorry to say, there was an administrative crisis—the president and all the vice presidents had resigned, so there was nobody to receive Branko. Branko was stubborn, however—Spielberg would not arrive if he did not get an assurance, even verbally, that there would be willingness to cooperate. Branko asked me who is in charge in a town when the president doesn't want to

---

*In Poland, cities have presidents, whereas in the United States they have mayors.

rule. My answer: "According to our system it is the city council of Kraków." Luckily the chairman of the city council, Kazimierz Barczyk, my old friend, was in town and received Branko in an office a few yards from the president's. We talked for an hour and left with the promise that was so important to Branko.

Nobody would have believed that just a few weeks ago Branko had undergone a serious heart operation. Years of work in the film industry takes a toll, and if one adds to it years spent in Auschwitz....I was a witness when Branko was asked if Spielberg's film would glorify Germans. Branko rolled up his sleeve and, showing a camp number tattooed on his forearm, answered, "Look! This is your guarantee!"

I knew about all the dramatic events in Branko's life, so I could not keep silent about his feelings and thoughts in connection with realizing* this film. A film about a good German? What about the saying, a good German is a dead German?

"Of course I know it," he answered. "In 1984 I was doing *The Winds of War* and found myself in Auschwitz again for the first time since the war. It was a strange experience. The emptiness of the camp made a big impression because when I was there before, the barracks were full of prisoners. Of course when we started working on the film I put the memories aside. After the war, I met many decent Germans. Many times I wondered why these good and decent people and their fellow countrymen from fifty years ago—let's say many of them—were people responsible for the crimes. The more I thought about it the less I understood. How can you understand people who have families, attend church regularly, eat meals at a family table, and suddenly—without explanation or cause—shoot their fellow creatures? This was the case with Amon Goeth, the commandant of the Płaszów Camp.

"I think it is not the fact that someone is good or bad, but

---

*In the film industry, the term *realizing* covers all the efforts involved in bringing a concept or, in this case a novel, to a fully completed film.

because all of a sudden one loses control over one's feelings and reactions. Circumstances in which people find themselves cause their reactions to become cruel or even murderous toward what is around them, and sometimes it is the opposite: someone surrounded by evil begins to oppose the evil. This is the case of Oskar Schindler, the hero of our film. In it we deal with two individuals from similar backgrounds and comparable opportunities. Both were fascinated by Hitler. But Amon Goeth was given an opportunity to kill. If he did not have such an opportunity maybe he would have been an honest carpenter or a shoemaker. Sometime ago I read a segment of a sermon by a German pastor who said, 'When Hitler began to persecute Communists, I did not protest because I was an anti-Communist. When Hitler started to persecute Jews, I did not protest because I was not Jewish. When he started persecuting activists in organizations, I did not protest because I did not belong to any organization. When he started to imprison and kill Catholic priests, I was silent because I was a Protestant, and when he started to come at me, there was no one left to take up my cause for me.'

"Maybe it is not an exact quote," said Branko, "but this was the essence of the sermon." "Most Germans," Branko continued, "were afraid to protest against the evil. Schindler, too, was afraid. He was frightened many times but he did something about it. No nation has evil in its genes, and therefore our film will be about a good German—Schindler—and about a bad German—Amon Goeth. From the viewpoint of orthodox morality, Oskar Schindler was not a man without faults. That he saved so many human beings is a fact that surely will tip the scale at the Last Judgment."

Our conversation returned to Branko Lustig's experiences in Auschwitz. He recalled that when filming *The Winds of War*, he worked with a German film crew. They were young people who would have been no more than four or five when the war ended.

"Before we started the cameras rolling, our director [Dan Curtis], an American, asked for a moment of silence because he wanted to say a prayer. He asked in this prayer that the souls of all who died on those desolate fields would let us make the film, which was dedicated to them. During that prayer, I looked at the faces of those young people—the cameraman, his assistants, electricians, the whole crew—they all were crying. I thought, Who knows, maybe some of them, if they were to find themselves in similar circumstances, would act just like the commandant of the Auschwitz camp, Rudolf Hoess. Lucky for them, they were born too late for fate to put them to such a test. Look at my country, the former Yugoslavia. Today a neighbor shoots at a neighbor though everybody who has known him for a half century thought he was a good person. There are no bad Croats or good Croats, bad Serbs or good Serbs. Circumstances caused them to act this way or that way. Oskar Schindler belonged to those people who reacted positively in adverse circumstances."

"How did you learn about Schindler for the first time?" I asked.

"Right after the book was published, in 1982. I already wanted to produce the film. At first Metro-Goldwyn-Mayer was interested. When I found out that Steven Spielberg would direct, I went to him and said, 'I want to work with you on this film.'

'Really?' he said.

'Yes,' I said.

'Why?' he asked.

"I rolled up my sleeve and silently showed him my number.... I was accepted."

3

About Schindler, Marta and Rosner's Violin

There are more than one hundred speaking roles in *Schindler's List*. All the main roles and most of the supporting ones were cast several months before the shooting began. As each role was cast, Magdalena Szwarcbart posted photos of the actors on a bulletin board. The space next to the character of Victoria Klonowska remained empty for a long time. Finally, a few days before shooting began, I met the actress selected to play Victoria. It was Małgosia Gebel, who has been living in Berlin for several years. After she finished acting school in Warsaw, she worked as a newscaster on Polish radio. Late in 1981 she went to Berlin to do a report about Polish refugees in Germany and remained there during the period of martial law.* At first she

---

*The period of martial law, called *Stan Wojenny* in Polish, was from 1981 to 1984. It was really the Polish Communist government's response to the Solidarity movement, though the public excuse was that an invasion of Poland by Russia was impending. During this time some leaders of Solidarity, including Walesa, were arrested, all passports were canceled, telephones disconnected, and newspapers closed for a few years. Most countries extended the visas for those who happened to have been visiting outside of Poland at the time.

worked as a newscaster, but later she returned to the occupation for which she trained—acting. In addition to leads in a seven-segment BBC television serial and a film by Rudolf Thome, she played Rosa Luxemburg in *Angry Harvest* (1985) by Agnieszka Holland, director of *Europa, Europa*. Ms. Gebel tested for a part in *Indiana Jones* but did not get it. Now she was cast in Spielberg's *Schindler's List*.

Victoria Klonowska really existed: She was one of Oskar Schindler's secretaries. Everything points to the fact, however, that Keneally gave Victoria the characteristics of another friend of Schindler, Marta. Marta lives near New York City, and I met her in December 1992, thanks to a good friend of mine, Janina Olszewska, who lives in Kraków. My friendship with Janina stems from the time when my article about Oskar Schindler appeared in *Dziennik Polski* [Polish Daily]. After reading that piece, Janina phoned to tell me that she had known Oskar Schindler well during the war, that he not only saved Jews but also helped many Polish people. She and her relatives were excellent examples. Janina invited me to visit her if I was interested. Of course I was.

An older, very distinguished lady opened the door of a small apartment in a stone house near the center of Kraków. A few old paintings were on the walls. Coffee was served in old porcelain. I turned on my tape recorder and the tale began.

Janina had lived with her husband on an estate near Wilno.* When the war started her husband was among the first called up in the mobilization. His young wife remained behind alone, out in the country. He did not return home when the Red army rolled into Lithuania. After a while it was announced that a special commission in Wilno was accepting the names of those who wished to leave the occupation zone. Janina, her estate devastated and plundered, had no means of support, so she decided to go to Kraków to live with her father. She did not

---

*Wilno was a part of Poland before World War II. During the war it became a part of Lithuania.

know that her father had died after having been taken prisoner by the Germans.

Janina qualified for departure, spent two months in a transitional German camp, and finally arrived in Kraków. Unfortunately her parents' apartment was occupied by Germans, so she stayed with her in-laws, where she met Oskar Schindler. The circumstances were unusual. Schindler wanted to rent an apartment in a house belonging to Janina's in-laws, so he came to negotiate the rent. Usually, if Germans found an apartment they liked in General Gubernia [Occupied Poland] they simply requisitioned it. Therefore, Janina remembered their first meeting well—because she encountered a "different" German.

During one of his subsequent visits to pay the rent, Schindler was accompanied by a girlfriend, a Czech from Śląsk, who asked Janina where she was working. Janina told her the truth, that she was looking for work. Schindler's girlfriend [Marta] offered Janina an office position in her firm, which sold enamelware produced by Schindler's factory on ·Zabłocie Street. Janina didn't know anything about working in an office but decided to accept the offer. She sat down with a bookkeeping textbook and started reading. Eventually, she came to a page where it said that if someone had read to that point, he or she knew all about basic office work. She closed the book and began to preside over a desk. The others in the office were Marta, four Jews, and one *Volksdeutsche* woman [a person of German descent]. Marta and Janina became good friends.

Now, a year after that first conversation, I visit Janina again—this time with Małgosia Gebel, who wants to learn as much as possible about the person she will portray. Małgosia brings a bouquet of beautiful flowers,* and we sit down in comfortable

---

*Flowers seem particularly plentiful and inexpensive in Poland. One can buy them on the streets everywhere. It is simply a fundamen-

armchairs. As we drink excellent coffee the tale about Marta unfolds.

Marta was born in Zaolzie, Czechoslovakia.* Her grandmother's last name was Kawulok. Her mother remarried—this time to a Czech. Marta grew up in a large family but her parents chose to send her to a teachers college in the Czech part of Cieszyn. After earning her diploma she began teaching in a country school. In 1938, the Polish army marched in and Poland took over the Zaolzie region. Marta lost her job. To make ends meet she began to trade, crossing into Czechoslovakia through the "green border"† and bringing back stockings, which she could sell in Poland. She made a living, and others survived by similar activities. (I know a bit about it; my grandmother knows even more—all because I was born and raised near that border. I remember that after the war, Polish food supplies went across the Olza River and shoes, combs, and other goods came back to Poland.)

Marta became engaged. Just before the outbreak of the war someone warned her that the Polish police were interested in her frequent escapades over the border. Moreover, someone had

---

tal social grace to bring them to one's hostess on the occasion of a visit, to greet arriving friends with a bouquet, or to present flowers to the principals involved with any public performance or occasion.

*After 1918 Zaolzie was part of Czechoslovakia, although 60 percent of its population was Polish/Silesian. That is why the Polish army invaded Zaolzie—to bring these people back to their "homeland." Thus, it became a part of Poland until the outbreak of World War II, when Zaolzie, as well as Polish Silesia, became a part of Germany. The history of central Europe before World War II is punctuated by military actions such as these, resulting from bitter differences over which country "really owned" or controlled what territory and which people. In Europe, World War II became the largest contest fought over such issues.

†The so-called green border refers to the border areas located in the countryside, as opposed to places of formal crossing, such as roads and railroad tracks. A person could cross the border without challenge by going through remote fields or across mountains. Such areas were often green with foliage or grass, thus the term, *green border*.

seen her in Schindler's car. (She had met Schindler some time
before.) Anyway, after the warning Marta and her fiancé
decided to escape to Czechoslovakia. Chased by the Polish
police, Marta's fiancé was shot to death, and Marta was arrested
and imprisoned in Lvov. When Schindler arrived in Kraków,
just after the Germans entered the city, he went to Montelupich
Prison looking for Marta. He was positive that he would find
her there—but no. It was much later that Marta actually arrived
in Kraków and went to live with him. Still later, she moved to
her own apartment on Ujejskiego Street.

"What kind of relationship was there between Marta and
Schindler?" we ask in unison.

"Marta was simply in love with Schindler. No ulterior motives.
She had money from her store on Krakówska Street. Schindler
supplied the goods, but she did not use any of his money.

"When Schindler took over his small factory," Janina continues, "everybody laughed that all his fortune consisted of was
a Jew by the name of Bankier—one of the former owners of the
Rekord factory—and ten enamel pot covers."

Initially, because of a shortage of coke [a fuel from coal] to
fuel the furnaces, they could not even start production.
Schindler contacted a Mr. Mianowski, the director of the city gas
works, to borrow some coke. Director Mianowski arranged for
the delivery of a wagon of coke to start production. The loan
was soon repaid, but more importantly, when Mianowski was
later arrested by the Germans, Schindler secured his release,
and when the Mianowski family had no money for living
expenses, Schindler gave them financial assistance. He made
additional profits by selling part of the enamelware production
on the black market. Products made out of iron were regulated
and could be purchased only by presenting a coupon called an
*Eisenmark.** This provided an opportunity for illegal deals. No

---

*The *Eisenmark*, literally "iron mark," was issued only for defense-
related purposes. Civilians were forbidden to purchase iron products.
The mark is the unit of German currency.

wonder that Schindler let Marta run that part of the business. He trusted her—she was his best friend.

In her supervisory capacity, Janina often visited Schindler's enamel factory on Zabłocie Street. She remembers the main fabricating hall: "It was awesome. In addition to the machinery, there were stoves with large kettles of soup for the workers, and *at* the factory gate, peasant women from the villages had set up a virtual farmer's market to sell their produce." So it was— before the liquidation of the ghetto and before the formation of the Płaszów camp.

"The enamel factory was run by Oskar Schindler and that Jewish former owner, Mr. Bankier," recalls Janina. "These improbable partners looked like the comic heroes of some silent movie." Bankier, short and fat, and Schindler tall and slim—just like Mutt and Jeff." Janina always had to bargain with Bankier to obtain the most popular goods for her "business"—such as the pint mugs so important to peasants from the villages. She settled all monetary matters personally with Schindler. One day, people in contact with the Polish underground approached Janina with what had become for the resistance an everyday matter, but nonetheless one of great importance. The Polish partisans hiding out in the forests needed large kettles with which to cook and double-sized bowls to use as plates. Because what they required was nonstandard size, their order had to be handled as a special one. The kettles, in particular, had to be made by hand rather than mass-produced; kettles of that size were not routinely made. Typically, when goods had been delivered as agreed, Janina would meet with Schindler to settle the accounts. This time, when it came to paying for the special kettles and bowls, Schindler refused to take any money.

"But why?" Janina asked, "I received the goods."

"Yes, yes, I know. It's all for the Polish 'bandits' in the woods—the partisans."

Of course, she was surprised and shocked at his answer.

Janina continues serving good coffee and reminiscing. She remembers once when an acquaintance, a Polish housekeeper from Lubicz Street, came to her in tears—the Germans were taking her son to slave labor back in the Reich. Could Schindler intervene? He arranged the boy's release, employing him in the factory till the end of the war. Another time an escaped Polish prisoner from Auschwitz showed up at Janina's saying that he was a friend of her husband—but he had no papers. When Schindler was asked to help, he gave the man a job as a chauffeur. He also got Janina's husband out of a prisoner-of-war camp. Still later, her husband was arrested and sentenced to death for his work with the underground. "Again, Schindler saved him," says Janina—but that is another story.

Janina does not remember the exact date when Schindler told her that if something happened to him he would not want the Gestapo to lay their hands on some documents kept in the right-hand drawer of his desk. At the end of 1941, the Gestapo arrested Schindler and imprisoned him on Pomorska Street. He was suspected of double-crossing the authorities because of his strange contacts with the attaché of the German embassy in Turkey, his trips to Budapest, and his dealings with the Polish and Jewish people. Hearing of his arrest, Janina hurried immediately to Schindler's apartment. She gathered up the papers from the right drawer of his desk and hid them in the sofa without reading them. When Schindler returned after a few days and found out about the "safe" for his secret documents, he laughed as if it were a good joke.

Another time, three Germans showed up at Marta's office after proof that the firm was selling iron goods on the black market. It was obvious they wanted to nail Schindler and they did a lot of searching. Finally, they took Janina to some office on Rynek Główny [the Kraków main square] where seven guys began an interrogation. They yelled, terrorized her with threats, telephoned the Montelupich Prison to send a police van to take her to jail, and used a whole gamut of psychological tricks in an effort to break her. Janina realized that no confession would give her freedom. On the contrary, it would only bury Schindler and her deeper. Near the end of her endurance, she asked to meet privately with the chief of interrogations— she had something important to tell him. One of the guys got up and took her out.

The "important information" Janina wanted to convey was to propose a bribe to let her go. At first the German official shuddered. She repeated the question, "How much?" He answered, "Fifty thousand marks." They began to bargain. Janina was willing to give him five thousand; that was below his dignity. They finally settled for ten. The sum was delivered from Schindler the next day, as agreed, and Janina was released. Schindler also sent his car for her. Wanting to know all the details of the conversations, he listened intently and then said, "Extraordinary! I'll send the guy a case of champagne, too. That information is certainly worth a case of champagne."

Schindler had learned how much and whom to pay to secure the release of someone who had been arrested.

The end of war was near. In the east, the Germans were retreating before the Red Army. One day a German showed up in the office of the firm with a lot of coupons for iron goods intended for the Todt Organization, which was in charge of the forced labor details from Nazi prisons. It was a matter of many tons of enamelware: A lot of money could be made on the black market using the right supporting legal documents to distribute the goods. Schindler devised a scheme: he made up invoices for shipping to territories that would fall into the hands of the Red Army in a day or so. That way the goods could be siphoned off into the black market without a trace. Schindler used the profits to buy Jews from Amon Goeth at the Płaszów camp and place them in his factory.

One day Janina happened to be at the Zabłocie factory on business when Amon Goeth showed up. Goeth always struck fear in everyone. For him, shooting someone dead was as big a deal as spitting on the ground. As it turned out, the commander had come to visit Schindler's Jewish sub-camp (the only camp where no one was ever killed). Oskar Schindler asked Janina to assist him during the muster. Roll call was ordered, the workers lined up, and then Schindler insisted that Janina follow him and Goeth. She trembled with fear like the others, but went along. She will never forget the sight of the frightened Jews staring at Goeth. One never knew how he would react—he was so unpredictable. This time Amon Goeth killed no one. Afterwards, Janina reproached Schindler for subjecting her to such an experience. Schindler answered quietly, "Maybe thanks to your presence Amon did not kill anybody today."

It was after the war that Janina learned about Schindler's last achievement. She went dancing at a local establishment where the two Rosner brothers played: Henry, the violin, and Leopold, the accordion. They had survived the occupation thanks to Schindler. Henry asked Janina if she recognized him. Of course she did.

"And my violin?" he asked.

This surprised her. "The violin? What about the violin?"

"This is not an ordinary instrument." (Not because it was built by a famous violin maker but because it went through an unusual ordeal, just like its owner.)

Henry told her how he was sent to Auschwitz and how Schindler got him out—but without the violin. Henry complained: He missed his violin. A few days later Oskar Schindler delivered the violin—which he had "liberated" from Auschwitz also.*

Listening to Janina's tales about Schindler and Marta, Małgosia Gebel thinks that maybe Steven Spielberg should enlarge Victoria Klonowska's part in the film.

"When did you last see Marta?" I ask Janina.

"Marta went with Oskar Schindler to Brinnlitz in the fall of 1944. For some time we corresponded. Then we stopped for

---

*The Rosner violin was donated recently to the United States Holocaust Memorial Museum in Washington, D.C., by three of the surviving Schindler Jews.

many years. We saw each other again not long ago. For a very short time—just a few hours."

"What did you talk about? Schindler?"

"We did not talk at all. We looked at each other and we cried."

4

Attention! Quiet on the Set! Action!

The date for Steven Spielberg's third visit in Kraków changed several times. At first he was to arrive the fifth of January; later, around the fifteenth. Finally, he told his producers in Kraków, Branko Lustig and Lew Rywin, that he trusted them completely with the preparations and that he would fly in just before the start of shooting. The exact date of arrival was kept a deep secret. Lew Rywin gave conflicting information even to his closest coworkers. It was announced in the newspapers *Życie Warszawy* and *Gazeta Wyborcza* that Spielberg would be there on the evening of February 23. Others swore for sure that it would be the evening of February 24. As usual, the truth was somewhere in between. The airplane with Spielberg and his closest family—Kate Capshaw, his wife, and their five children— landed at Balice Airport at 8:20 in the morning, Wednesday, February 24, 1993. They were greeted by Jerry Molen, who had arrived a few days earlier, and by Branko Lustig and Lew Rywin. After a long flight from Los Angeles, Spielberg and his family wanted to rest at their residence in Wola Justowska, a suburb of Kraków. The house, on Zielony Dół [Green Dale] Street, was typically used for receptions honoring dignitaries visiting Kraków. It had been refurbished for Spielberg at a cost of $75,000. For the next three months it was to be his home as well as his workplace, because every day after returning from shooting *Schindler's List* he would work for several hours editing *Jurassic Park*, which was to premiere on June 11, 1993, and when that was finished, he would start editing *Schindler's List*.

In his new home Spielberg found a letter from Andrzej Wajda, who at that time was working in Japan. The letter accompanied a painting by the young Polish artist Janusz Klekot. Wajda presented the painting to Spielberg, noting that it contained several visual allusions to American films Spielberg would appreciate. Wajda also expressed the wish that the Polish film crews with whom Spielberg would be working for the first time would fully satisfy his every directorial desire, a proud tradition of crews in the Polish film industry.

One week before Spielberg's arrival in Kraków the producers received a new, revised, and completed version of the script for *Schindler's List*. Spielberg deleted several scenes from the end of the film but added some new ones. One of them would take place at the drugstore Apteka Pod Orłem, on Plac Zgody in the ghetto. The drugstore was managed by a Polish pharmacist, Tadeusz Pankiewicz.* Here the Jews from the Kraków ghetto received medical help, often without paying for it, and this was the contact point for the Polish and Jewish underground organizations. Tadeusz Pankiewicz was honored for his part in the Holocaust as one of the "Righteous Among the Nations" and awarded a medal by Yad Vashem, the Holocaust Memorial in Jerusalem. At first, Apteka Pod Orłem was not included in the script, though it figures prominently in the book.

---

*Those wishing to know more about this extraordinary man and the role he and his pharmacy played in helping the Jews of the ghetto may read of this in his book, *The Cracow Ghetto Pharmacy* by Tadeusz Pankiewicz. Translated from the Polish by Henry Tilles. New York: Holocaust Library, 1987. The original Polish text was published in Kraków in 1947 and reprinted in Israel in 1985.

Another addition to the script made by Spielberg was influenced by his talk with Andrzej Wajda during his first visit to Kraków. Wajda described a scene which he always wanted to incorporate in one of his films but never had the opportunity. It would show a hungry Jewish child trying to steal a roll from a bakery cart. Unfortunately the cart is protected by barbed wire. Spielberg was so impressed by the story that he wrote it into his script. It turned out later that this was not to be the last addition or correction.

The script for *Schindler's List* has a long history. The first version was prepared by Thomas Keneally, the author of the book. However, his script ended up being more suitable for a TV serial, so he was thanked and another scriptwriter was approached. No less than Kurt Luedtke was next. Kurt's excellent credits include an Oscar for the script of *Out of Africa,* which won seven Oscars in 1985—including Best Picture and Best Screenplay Adaptation. Luedtke, however, also did not succeed in adapting Keneally's book into a satisfactory film script. Spielberg had great respect for Luedtke's creativity, but with his efforts still failing to satisfy, Luedtke lost his enthusiasm for realizing *Schindler's List.* Around 1989 Steven Zaillian was approached. Zaillian had already successfully authored a script for *Awakenings* (1990).* Well, the third time's the charm— as the saying goes!

Spielberg brought with him not only changes of scenes but also additions of new elements, enriching existing scenes. He had obtained new material from the testimonies of witnesses and from lectures. There were two pages of such notes,† which

---

*Other writing credits for Steven Zaillian include *Searching for Bobby Fischer* (1993), *Jack the Bear* (1993), *Clear and Present Danger* (1994), *Twister* (1996), *Mission: Impossible* (the story) (1996), *Amistad* (1997), and *A Civil Action* (1998). Mr. Zaillian also has editing credits and directed *Searching for Bobby Fischer.* He will direct *A Civil Action.*

†The full text of these notes is reproduced at the end of the chapter. That complete version of the notes is important for what it reveals about the level of detail at which Steven Spielberg works. The

were prepared by Sergio Mimica-Gezzan, one of the assistant directors, several hours before shooting began.

The different departments—scenery, wardrobe, props, special effects, production—had only a few hours to get ready. It was difficult to reach anyone by phone. When I called the production office, I was put on hold and listened to a ragtime tune from the film *The Sting*. Usually, one had to listen to at least one refrain. During the hours just before day one I must have listened to a few dozen repeats until finally I got Kasia Trocka on the line.

"What's new?" I asked (an original question!).

"I heard the answer of a worn-out Kasia. "Jeez, I don't know, what's new?"

"Where is 'the Master'?" (This is the insider's code name by which we refer to Spielberg.)

"Everywhere."

"You mean like a god!?"

"No, but he is moving without stopping to rest. He may be in the Liban quarry or maybe somewhere else. Everything is changing from minute to minute. We got a new version of the script. There're about ninety pages to be rewritten or thrown out—three-quarters of the last version. That's what we're doing."

In the evening I drove up to the Hotel Piast, where the film's production offices were housed. Yugoslav trucks were unloading beautiful old automobiles borrowed from the museum in Lubljana: three Mercedes and a huge luxurious Horche. Katarzyna (Kasia) is still at the computer making corrections. By the time I left, snow was falling. Bartek, Lew Rywin's black

---

notes, and their annotations alerting various production departments to work they must do before the shoot begins, reveal the level and accuracy of research he conducted before beginning to film. The details planned in these notes are accurate reflections of details one can find within photos, films, and eyewitness accounts of the Holocaust.

schnauzer, was jumping around like crazy in the fresh snow with
a new friend, Hamlet, a short-haired dachshund. The next day I
was told that Bartek was out the whole night—but he returned
in the morning. Well, he was lonely. No one had time to play
with him.

People in the office worked until the wee hours in the
morning to get ready for the first "clap."* On February 26, the
five-day weather forecast for southern Poland began like this:
For the next two days—heavy clouds, occasional snow, some
clearing; maximum temperature 30° to 33°F, minimum 28° to
31°F; wind moderate to changing. Starting in March it was to be
even cooler. After two nice sunny and warm days—Saturday
and Sunday—the first day of filming was freezing cold. At 6:00
A.M. my outdoor thermometer at home showed 28°F.

The work schedule for March 1, 1993, the first of seventy-five
planned days, called for the extras to show up at 5:00 A.M.
(before sunrise) in the wardrobe department, which was set up
in the TV Studio for Art Programs in Łęg, a Kraków suburb.
Breakfast would be served at 6:00 A.M. Shooting will begin at
8:30 A.M. Branko Lustig went to meet the extras. He needed two
hundred people and five hundred showed up. That was too
many for the set, so three hundred were sent home that day.

The first take was for scene 75: cleaning the snow in front of
Schindler's factory on Lipowa Street by a group of Jews who
worked in the factory, Deutsche Emailwaren Fabrik [German
Enamelware Factory]. Activities such as cleaning the streets of
snow or mud were organized by the Germans starting January
5, 1940, during the first winter of the occupation. That day
three hundred Jews and twenty trash wagons were used. A year

---

*The clap referred to is the clap of the slate board which is used in
front of the camera at the beginning of each take to provide a
reference label and a means for sound and image synchronization.
The clap is made by clapping a pivoted piece like a ruler down across
the top of the board to provide a quick, sharp sound to link with the
frame image, showing the moment of contact.

later all the Jews sixteen and older had to spend twelve days before the end of January cleaning the streets. Each workday had to be verified by a stamp from the *Judenrat*. Whoever did not have twelve stamps on their *Kennkarta* by January 31 automatically lost permission to live in Kraków and, in reality, was deported to a concentration camp.

Scene 75 occurs in the winter of 1941. Winters were supposedly much colder then, but today, too, the temperature is below freezing, making crystals in the air. After standing in the snow for several hours one really is frozen to the bone, and what about the extras playing those Jews dressed in threadbare rags and no gloves?

The first take for *Schindler's List* was on Poselska Street next to the former prison called Św. Michała [St. Michael's]. The Germans took it over on September 6, 1939, right after entering Kraków. On September 13 thirty-two persons were executed, twenty-five of them Jewish. They were rounded up from houses on nearby Grodzka Street. Poldek Pfefferberg's parents lived here, at 48 Grodzka Street, a short distance from the corner of Poselska Street, where Poldek met Oskar Schindler for the first time. Schindler came to see Mrs. Pfefferberg, an interior decorator, about redoing his newly acquired apartment. Steven Spielberg changed Keneally's description of that meeting. For the first meeting between Schindler and Poldek, he chose Marjacki Bazylika, where they take advantage of the asylum of a holy place to close their first deal.

Allan Starski, the production designer, did not have to change much for this particular scene. A pink modern awning over a men's clothing store had to be removed, a few period signs were placed on walls of buildings, and a round kiosk for handbills and posters was built. I remember one such round kiosk that was on Piłsudski Street across from Czapski Museum, but by the end of the sixties all those kiosks disappeared from the streets in Kraków, and now they had to be reconstructed for the film. Today's scene, however, required a lot of work from the production crew for other reasons: They had to bring many trucks of fresh snow. The last two days had been sunny and the snow melted fast. There was a lot of snow though—nice white snow—at the airport in Balice, not the dirty gray kind like that in the Błonia meadows. Several truckloads of snow also arrived from Zakopane, the famous skiing resort in the High Tatra Mountains. It was ordered earlier, when there was no snow in Kraków, but the order could not be canceled in time and the snow arrived "according to contract."

Jerry Molen arrives on the set at 7:15 A.M. to join Branko Lustig, Lew Rywin, and Allan Starski. Steven Spielberg arrives fifteen minutes later. It takes time to set up the cameras. One is in the middle of Poselska Street on a tall crane; the other is on the balcony of one of the houses. A group of extras is waiting on the street. The actors arrive at 8:15. Among them is Ben Kingsley, the unforgettable Gandhi, who plays Itzhak Stern—Oskar Schindler's head bookkeeper. Among the Polish actors I notice Aldona Grochal playing Mrs. Nussbaum.

Beata Paluch plays Mancy Rosner, the wife of Henry Rosner, a Kraków violinist. Jacek Wójcicki, one of the cabaret performers who "tried out" for the film in Piwnica Pod Baranami [The Cellar under the Rams] during Spielberg's first visit to Kraków, plays Henry Rosner. The director begins a run-through. Spielberg observes the first take through the camera viewfinder. Later takes he will view on the black-and-white video monitor mounted next to the camera. Then, Janusz Kamiński, in charge of photography, will take his place behind the camera.

Janusz Kamiński was born in Ziembice, Poland. In 1980 he left for the United States to study in the Department of Fine Arts and Film at Columbia College in Chicago. Later he transferred to Los Angeles and received a scholarship to the American Film Institute. He began his film career in 1987 with the film *The Fallen Angel*. Subsequently he was director of photography for *Grim Prairie Tales* (1990), *The Rain Killer* (1991), and *Trouble Bound* (1992). Janusz Kamiński also worked on *The Adventures of Huckleberry Finn* (1993) and on two films for television, *Class of '61* (1993) and *Wildflower* (1991), produced by Amblin Entertainment, Spielberg's production firm. The official title for Janusz Kamiński on this film is director of photography, but that does not mean Janusz always stands behind the camera. His responsibilities are many. He sets the light levels, decides on the choice of lenses, and determines the positions of the cameras. Yes, sometimes he operates the camera, but most of the time it is his assistant who is the cameraman—Raymond Stella, or simply Ray. He, in turn, has an assistant cameraman who sets lens adjustments for distance and aperture. His name is Steve Tate.

Steve is an independent cameraman who wanted to work on *Schindler's List* so much that he proposed to Jerry Molen that he would work for free and said he would take anything for a job, even sweeping the floor. "I cannot let you do that," Jerry answered, "but I have an opening for an assistant cameraman." The camera, as well as all the filmmaking equipment, is rented from a well-known German firm, Arri, which produces the world-famous Arriflex cameras. On the right side of the camera there is a sticker with a motto from Hemingway: "Only something you are unsure of can be the nucleus for a great work." Glued to the camera on the other side, where Steve sits, there is a photo of his five-month-old son.

In scene 75 a group of Jews from Schindler's factory is escorted by guards. They march straight at the camera in two lines. A German military car drives up. A German officer jumps out. A military truck with snow-cleaning equipment stops. The Jewish workers crowd the truck, picking up shovels or brooms. First rehearsal, then a second. Finally the director gives a sign to start shooting. Marek Brodzki, assistant to the director, gives a loud command: "Attention! Quiet on the set! ACTION!" Everybody moves according to the director's instructions. Two seconds later Spielberg, who is observing the picture on the

monitor, gives the command to the camera operator: "Action!"
The camera starts. There is silence on the set except for the
loud orders in German: "Schnell! Schnell!" [Faster! Faster!]
Several Jewish policemen leading the groups of Jewish workers
listen subserviently to the orders of the German officer, then
they in turn force the workers to shovel snow, pushing them
with heavy wooden nightsticks. I look at my watch, it is exactly
8:30 A.M., precisely as it was planned on the schedule for the
day. After a while another command from the director: "Cut!"
The whole thing lasted less than a minute. Scene 75 is finished.
The first of 349.

On the same set, scenes 77 and 79. German guards shoot a
one-armed Jewish worker, Lowenstein. Henryk Bista plays the
part. The Germans cannot understand how it is possible that
Schindler's worker is so "necessary for the war effort"—with
only one arm. The special-effects man glues a small piece of
metal on Henryk Bista's forehead. The device has an explosive
which will fracture a capsule of artificial blood, but it is
arranged so as to prevent any injury to Henryk's forehead. A
shot. Lowenstein/Bista falls face down on the snow. Red blood
shows up well on the sparkling white snow, only it will photograph black on the black-and-white film.

In the afternoon we move to Szeroka Street. At the end of the
short street between Dajwor and Szeroka streets in Kraków's
Kazimierz district a gate and a fragment of the ghetto wall was
reconstructed. The real ghetto was in Podgórze on the right
bank of the Wisła River, but between the Wisła, Podgórski
Rynek [Square], Lwowska Street, and Krzemionki, the topogra-
phy of that part of Kraków changed—new streets, new modern
buildings, including a glass high-rise next to Plac Zgody*—so
Spielberg chose the Szeroka Street and neighborhood to build
his own replica of a ghetto.

---

*These streets and locations are within what was the actual ghetto,
but because of the changes mentioned here, the film set had to be built
elsewhere to achieve the correct "look" and skyline.

Szeroka Street itself is not to be filmed today, therefore the production crew used it for the production support and property vehicles: antique Mercedes cars; minibuses to serve as dressing rooms for the stars; and a large bus for the production office, complete with a fax machine. That bus, too, could be a dressing room. There is also a large tent which will be used as a dining room for all involved. The first day, a catering firm from Yugoslavia set up a buffet with a choice of beef, chicken, potatoes, pasta, and vegetables. In the tent there are tables with salads, fruit, yogurt, and pastries. There is also mineral water and juices. Spielberg's table is always the second one from the entrance. There his wife Kate joins him for meals. Evidently he eats only because she insists—and usually just some vegetables. Others have rather big appetites.

After an hour's break, during which the technical crew sets up rails for the camera dolly, we move on to shooting a scene at the set piece for the ghetto gateway.

Set-up 1: German officers, including Amon Goeth, ride into the ghetto.
Set-up 2: Poldek Pfefferberg leaves the ghetto. Poldek runs in front of the streetcar and jumps onto the rear platform.

The same electric streetcars that were in use before the war continued in use up through part of the sixties. The doors did not close automatically, and the conductor sat at the rear door and sold and canceled tickets. First they retired the conductors, and later the old cars, though there were some old cars preserved in the historical division of MPK [*Miejskie Przedsiębiorstwo Komunikacyjne* (City Office of Transportation)], which rented out to the film an old streetcar together with conductor uniforms and the original tickets.

During the war, tram number 6 went from Wieliczka Street onto Lwowska Street, to Plac Zgody, over III Most [the Third

Bridge], along Starowiślna Street, to Rynek Główny [the main square of Kraków], and along Zwierzyniecka Street to the Salwator suburb. It crossed the ghetto on Lwowska to the III Most. Poldek used to jump onto the streetcar and ride to the Aryan side. A young Israeli actor, Jonathan Sagalle, plays Poldek. He is unknown to film audiences in Poland and the United States but very popular in Israel and Germany. His film roles were in *The Little Drummer Girl* (1984), *Remembrance of Love* (TV, 1982), and *Nauga* a.k.a. *Drifting* (1983). For the latter he received the best actor and the King David's Harp prize in Israel. He also acts in a popular Israeli television serial, *Lemon Popsicle*.

I befriended Jonathan (I call him by his Polish name, (Jonasz) early on because he plays a person dear to my heart. Jonasz, whose family comes from Będzin, Poland, was born in Canada but lives in Israel. He speaks a little Polish. Actually, he knows a few Polish expressions that his grandmother taught him, such as the Polish equivalent for "Don't give me the business." We became acquainted in the Forum Hotel a day before the shooting of *Schindler's List* began. Steven Spielberg had invited all participants for evening cocktails. The stars arrived: Liam Neeson, Ben Kingsley. Anna Maria Stein, unit publicist for *Schindler's List*, introduced Jonathan to me. We spoke English during the party. At one point Jonasz started to repeat each sentence I spoke. I thought he did not understand me so I repeated the sentence and he repeated it again, then I, again, just like a broken record. I could not understand why he would be so impolite as to mimic me. Finally, he explained: He plays his part speaking English but he is supposed to be a young Jew in Kraków in 1939. He would not be speaking English like his cousin in New York. His English would need to have an Eastern European accent, and he noticed that the way I pronounced my *h* had the Eastern European flavor. That's how I was "caught" to be a private dialect coach for Jonathan Sagalle. I recorded for him all the lines which he says in the film several times— sometimes fast, sometimes slower. I had never realized that my study of phonetics at the university might be useful some day.

During the first day of filming, Spielberg completed nine scenes of *Schindler's List*. That evening I phoned Los Angeles. I wanted to tell Poldek that his life's dream had come true. Poldek wanted to be present at the beginning of filming, but a few weeks earlier he entered a clinic for heart trouble. He was not home. His wife Mila—also a character in the film—answered the phone.

"Where is Poldek?" I ask.

"What do you mean, 'Where?'" Mila answers. "At work."

I hesitate. "But I understood...well...his heart...."

"So what," says Mila. "You know him. He's a workaholic. He decided he had enough of the hospital stay. He has too many things to take care of."

The next day, when I met Niusia Karakulska, another character in the film, I told her about Poldek's heart problems and how he took care of them. She recalled a saying of her mother, Regina Horowitz—something of a reassurance in the face of adversity: "If Hitler could not finish me, nobody can; nothing can happen to me."

The following memo is an example of the level of detail at which Spielberg works (see footnote on page 46).

SCHINDLER'S LIST—MEMO

FROM: Sergio
TO: All Concerned   [Feb. 28, 1993]
RE: Most Recent Notes from Steven

Please be aware of the following if it affects you:

In Płaszów Camp we'll see (in background of some scenes) Ukrainian guards punishing people by systematic *whipping*. We ought to make a few dummy whips for that (I believe we don't have any). Also, along with the truncheons we already have, we should get some real whips for the guards to carry. (ART/SFX/PROPS/M-UP)*

Let's discuss a possibility of having a *PA system* at Płaszów Camp and on the Cracow streets for playing live the announcements made by the Germans over the loudspeakers. Should we pre-record a voice in German? (SOUND/ART/OSSI)†

In Płaszów Camp, we'll see a *girl carrying a cow-bell* on her belt as a punishment for her attempted escapes (one hundred other prisoners executed as a result of it). (WB‡/PROPS/CASTING)

In Płaszów, prisoners often *washed their hair in "coffee,"* that being the only hot liquid available. (PROPS/HAIR)

In the ghetto raid, a huge pile of luggage is built up on the Peace Square [Plac Zgody or Zgoda Square] twice a man's height. I suggest cardboard boxes covered with luggage. (ART/PROPS)§

In Płaszów (Health Action and Depot)‖ we'll see SS Aufseherin [female overseer] Frau Orłowska (an extra, tall blond) with a whip. (CASTING/PROPS/WB/MAKEUP)

In Płaszów kitchen, there is a German woman overseer, a master of [the] whip, big, fat, and commanding, with rows and rows (50?) of women peeling potatoes and onions. (ART/WB/PROPS/MAKEUP/CASTING)

---

*These notations in parenthesis call out the departments who need to act on the basis of the note. Here, for example, they would be art direction, special effects, properties, and makeup.

†Ossi Ragheb is a language consultant and dialogue coach for the film.

‡Wardrobe.

§The suggestion is to create a basic pile of cardboard boxes only veneered with the luggage. This approach is often used in scenery and dressing elements to reduce the number of individual pieces that must be handled as well as the number of actual period props required to support the desired visual effect.

‖Refers to two specific scenes in the script.

In the ghetto raid, Pfefferberg notices blood on German soldiers (like surgeons [covered with blood during an operation]) that catch him in the street. Also there: Dogs with Goeth should be attempting to attack Pfefferberg so the SS have to hold them back. Have police dogs there as well as Rolf and Ralf. (WB/MAKEUP/PRODUCTION)

Goeth has a bodyguard. Grun, a wrestler. (WB/CASTING/MAKEUP)

At Płaszów Health Action, one of the banners should say: "For Each Man a Fit Occupation." (ART)

In the same Action, naked people were allowed to carry their clothes over the arm. (WB/PROPS) Doctors are looking for skin disease, pimples, marks—as signs of imperfection and thus selecting people for either work or transport. (MAKEUP)

Goeth sometimes wears white gloves. (WB)

At Prokocim Depot, labels and tags on luggage should have real Jewish names from our existing lists. There will be a close angle. (PROPS)

Songs played on the gramophone are: "Mummy, Buy Me a Pony" and "Gute Nacht, Mutti." (PRODUCTION/SOUND/PROPS)

At nightclub, Schindler and Nazis sing a song. (PRODUCTION/SOUND)

Explore possibility of finding a location for a ghetto hospital ward, overlooking a ghetto street for a raid scene. (LOCATIONS/ART)

In the raid, the FRANTIC WOMAN and the OLD MAN should speak English. (CASTING)

In Płaszów, women's barracks, wedding scene, have a makeshift ring for Rebecca (a faucet washer or made from a bullet shell casing). (PROPS)

Helen Hirsch will be established in the exodus and at the arrival in the ghetto. (MAKEUP/HAIR/WB/CASTING)

In the ghetto raid, there will be a scene where 150 men are made (by the SS) to run a race to the Peace Square with a promise that the fastest 75 men will be allowed to go to work in Płaszów. At the arrival line, the SS count off the first 75, then jump to round up the "losers" for transport.

Also here, SS, in order to save on bullets, line up 6 people (among them 88, GHETTO GIRL) one behind the other and shoot as many as they can with one shot. The two last men survive, the bullet having penetrated only four. SS shoot them down. (SFX/WB/STUNTS)

Schindler's men are back in sc. 316—seeing the women arrive.

cc: Branko, Jerry, Lew, Michał S., Bonnie, Nada, Miki, Allan, Jan Janik, Michael H., Batia, Anna, Ron, Ossi, Lucky, Christina, Judy, Bruce, Marek B, Krzysztof Z., Magda

5

The Dispute About
Auschwitz-Birkenau

The last kilometer leading to the location in front of the camp in
Birkenau was crowded with automobiles, busses, and trucks. All
together about sixty vehicles transported actors, extras, electricians, scenic crews, wardrobe, catering, and others. The company traffic had to stop and park at the viaduct, which was
guarded by the highway patrol. They let me park my car nearby
as well. Never before was it guarded so well.

Outside and in front of the gate leading to Auschwitz-
Birkenau a camp had been reconstructed—really, just a portion
of one. It looked like a mirror image of a fragment of the actual
Birkenau camp. There were only ten days in which to build it,
but the carpenters hired for the project came from the Podhale
Mountains, where everything is built of wood, and so they were
experts in building wooden structures in no time.* When
Spielberg arrived in Kraków, the set already had been con-

---

*This book makes clear that the producers of *Schindler's List*
economized in facilitating their production needs by hiring "special-
ists" to perform certain tasks. Fast, sturdy carpentry is noted here;
later we read that when TV antennas had to be removed from steep
Kraków rooftops, the workers were brought from a Polish mountain
region where everyone is an expert mountain climber, and so on.

structed. All it needed was a coat of paint on the barracks, concrete posts with barbed wire, and some dirt on the asphalt road to make it look less modern.

A month and a half earlier, Spielberg had secured permission from all the authorities to film several precisely specified scenes in the authentic places in the camp proper from March 4 to 6— but all of a sudden those plans fell into jeopardy.

Sunday, January 17, I received a phone call from some friends in New York. They had read in the *New York Times* that the World Jewish Congress objected to Spielberg's filming activity in the camp. Several hours later I received a fax from the Reuters agency:

> The World Jewish Congress is trying to prevent Steven Spielberg from using the Auschwitz death camp as a setting in his new film. Kalman Sultanik, vice president of the organization, disclosed last Friday that he registered a protest with the Polish embassy in the United States against Spielberg's plans and declared that he will take up the matter with the Polish authorities in Warsaw at the end of the month.
>
> The Jewish Congress leaders are afraid that the unrestricted activities of a commercial filming crew on the site where more than a million Jews were exterminated during World War II will desecrate the place.

I visited Branko Lustig in his apartment, which is also his office. Branko was bedridden—doctor's orders—since he twisted his ankle returning from a trip to Los Angeles, where he had been consulting with Spielberg. Branko was frustrated because he had in front of him a letter from four months ago, signed by the director of the World Jewish Congress, E. Steinberg, in which he stated that he had no objections whatsoever to filming several scenes for *Schindler's List* on the grounds of the Auschwitz camp. "I was a prisoner in this camp for two years," said Branko, "I know the German fascists well and I would be the last one to permit any kind of desecration of that place. I am also looking at it from another viewpoint. I knew Germans who submitted to the fascist ideology and at the same time tried to preserve their own personal humanity in those inhuman times. Oskar Schindler was such a man. Today, when we see hundreds of thousands of Germans marching with lighted candles protesting neo-Nazism, I always think that Schindler was such a man—one who carried a lighted candle alone during the war. We should not forget that lonely candle. That would be profane —the profaning of the truth and of history," concluded Branko.

There was an impasse concerning filming in Auschwitz. Marvin Levy, press agent for Steven Spielberg, explained in vain that rumors about Spielberg's intentions to build a replica of a gas chamber on the camp proper were unfounded. All the explanations did not change Kalman Sultanik's stand. He insisted that no one consulted him concerning the script and he was unsuccessful in his endeavors to contact Spielberg.

When shown the documents agreeing to the filming locale signed by the executive director of the World Jewish Congress, Kalman Sultanik changed his tune. He protested in the name of the International Council of the State Museum in Auschwitz. That organization was to look into the matter of the filming for *Schindler's List* during a meeting scheduled for the beginning of February.

After two days of discussions, the International Council of the State Museum in Auschwitz published a document which stated that they were concerned about the preparations for filming *Schindler's List* in the Auschwitz-Birkenau camp. They agreed that taking up such a topic as the annihilation of Jews in the Auschwitz camp has its purpose, but some prior experiences in working with the filming of fictional stories made them fear that authenticity would not be adhered to and the sanctity of the place would be violated. Spielberg was asked to limit filming in the camp proper to documentary footage, and that any scenes pertaining to story telling or pictorial portrayal requiring decorations, change in terrain, or use of a large number of extra actors take place outside the camp.

Spielberg did not care to cause tensions over the filming of a few scenes—only three days of filming out of seventy-five planned for Poland. Soon the Reuters agency announced that Spielberg would meet in New York with the representatives of the International Council of the State Museum in Auschwitz and representatives of the World Jewish Congress in order to establish the criteria for an understanding in the matter of filming in Birkenau.

After the meeting, which took place on February 11, he abandoned the idea of filming on the grounds of the former camp. Instead he decided to build a fragment of the camp in front of the gate to Birkenau. Six barracks which were to be used in the reconstructed Płaszów camp were taken apart and reconstructed near the train spur to Birkenau but outside the former camp, though the historic Auschwitz gate and some of the original barracks in the women's camp were still to serve as backgrounds.

There would be five scenes filmed in Birkenau: the arrival of the three hundred Schindler women in Birkenau; the selection by Dr. Mengele; the bath; a night in the barrack featuring Mila Pfefferberg; and finally the departure of the whole group of three hundred Jewish women who were on the Schindler list.

The release of three hundred women from Auschwitz could only have occurred with the knowledge and permission of the commander of the camp, Rudolf Hoess. How was it arranged? There was a lot of hearsay about this. I asked one of Schindler's girlfriends, Marta, how it was really accomplished. She told me that a lot of money and a very attractive woman who was the go-between to handle the bribes played a big part. My friend Janina suggested that this woman was Liza Kine, one of Schindler's secretaries. She was a beautiful woman, tall, blond, and slightly plump. "She might have been the one," said Janina.

Janina had more to tell about Liza—an incident that was as revealing of the climate of paranoia in occupied Poland as it was of a little-known side of the Führer himself. Liza had a German fiancé who worked on the staff that surrounded Hitler, though he himself was anti-Hitler. One day, visiting in Kraków, he told a story in Janina's presence about Hitler. Upset by the happenings on the front, he supposedly threw himself on the floor and kicked his legs in a tantrum like a child. Liza interrupted her fiancé, saying, "Be careful what you tell us, after all, Janina is a Polish woman; she might have to turn you in." Listening to this, Janina felt kind of embarrassed, but the young man was not bothered and continued telling stories about the Führer. We must remember, though, that the Germans always held the Poles under suspicion, so to turn in a "traitor" or a Jew was often a matter of self-protection. Liza remained Schindler's secretary till the end of the war.

From that fragment in history, as well as the Spielberg film, I became acquainted with several personalities: first of all, Mila Pfefferberg (Page), Poldek's wife; also Edzia Wertheim, from New York City; Stella Müller-Madej and Niusia Karakulska, from Kraków; and Niusia's brother Ryszard Horowitz, again from New York City. Ryszard is the hero of one of the most dramatic episodes of the film. In that scene he is five years old. Together with his father, Dolek Horowitz, his six-year-old cousin, Olek Rosner, and uncle, Henry Rosner, they find themselves in Birkenau. The Gestapo had sent them there from Schindler's factory in Brinnlitz while Schindler was away. Ryszard's mother, Regina Horowitz, was leaving Birkenau for Schindler's factory in Brinnlitz when she saw her husband and son behind the barbed wires, though she had thought for sure they were safe at Schindler's. Now, her happiness on leaving the Birkenau nightmares was shattered by a new fear—for the lives of her loved ones.

After the end of the war, Regina returned to Kraków with her daughter Niusia, convinced that their loved ones were dead; they even met some witnesses who thought they had died. One day Regina and her daughter went to a movie. Before the feature film they saw a documentary about Auschwitz with scenes from the liberation, and Regina recognized Ryszard among the 180 liberated children. He was alive! A few days searching resulted in finding Ryszard with his surrogate family in Kraków.

Ryszard grew up and was educated in Kraków. In 1959 he was a student in graphics at the Kraków ASP [Academia Sztuk Pięknych (Academy of Fine Arts)], and he received a stipend to study in the United States of America. His first great break came when he had an opportunity to photograph Eleanor Roosevelt, which opened the door to a great career in the field of photography. After thirty years of hard work backed by his acknowledged talent, he belongs among America's top photographers. In 1963, while still a student, he received a prestigious award from a New York organization of commercial graphic artists. In 1991 he was awarded a prize for the most creative research in photography based on computer technology.

When he came to Kraków in 1989 to attend the opening of an exhibition of his work, we spoke about his life and art. I asked him if he told his sons about his episode in the camp. "No," he answered, "they are too young." As a prisoner in Auschwitz though, he was younger than his older son Daniel is now.

A few months ago I visited Ryszard in his New York studio where he was finishing his latest commercial project. Several top male and female models were milling about. When they left we returned to our conversation about his personal experiences in survival and about Spielberg's *Schindler's List*. Ryszard told me about a certain New York medical center that conducts examinations of people who survived the Holocaust. The scientists want to discover if the stress experienced by the victims might have produced genetic changes which could influence heredity. There is some evidence that such changes are possible. "However, it appears that I am an absolute exception," Ryszard Horowitz says, smiling. "That horrible experience did not leave a stamp on me." After a while he added, "If it were possible, I should like my son to play my part in Spielberg's film. It would be an excellent closure to my history."

Ryszard's son was not cast for the part in the film. A Polish teenager, Michał Babiarz, plays young Ryszard, and six-year-old Kamil Krawiec portrays Ryszard's cousin, Olek Rosner. Also taking part in the *Schindler's List* Auschwitz scenes are several Israeli actresses: Embeth Davidtz, Adi Nitzan, Miri Fabian, as well as Polish actors and actresses Jacek Wójcicki, Olaf Lubaszenko, Aldona Grochal, Beata Paluch, and Beata Nowak. About five hundred extras were also employed.

The makeup call for the first actresses is for 5:30 A.M. They are picked up from the hotel an hour earlier for their trip to the location site. Shooting is scheduled for 10:00 A.M., but the sun does not shine through the clouds and fog of the winter day. Before the shooting, Spielberg pays a brief private visit to the monument for Auschwitz victims and places a bouquet of flowers. This will be one of the most difficult days for the stars, extras, and the crew. Everybody envies the engineer of the locomotive pulling six wagons for the women's transport to Brinnlitz. He is sitting in a cozy warm cab.

One of the women's barracks constructed for the set has a heating system. Most of the extras are crowded in there while waiting for their cues. I join them to warm up. There I meet several friends who are making some additional money as extras. One of them, sporting an imposing beard, is Zbyszek. He is a conservator of art in a museum, but there is a slow period in his work, so he works for Spielberg. The barracks are filled with men because the women are being loaded into the wagons.

This is to be one of the most dramatic scenes: The German guards are separating a mother from her daughter. Miri Fabian, an Israeli actress, plays Mrs. Dresner, and her daughter Danka is portrayed by a Polish sixth grader—Ania [diminutive for Anna] Mucha. Miri Fabian is a wonderful actress. The scene is so moving that even many of the seasoned crew members cannot watch. Spielberg directs that one camera be placed on the watchtower and another one be taken off the tripod and carried by hand. He is standing next to the cameraman, surrounded by the crowd of female extras. At one moment Miri Fabian, playing Mrs. Dresner, disappears among the crowding women. "Keep looking for her," Spielberg tells the cameraman. Such takes by a handheld camera are reminiscent of documentary film, and Steven will use that technique often in this film.

Noontime. The caterers pass around mugs of hot tea. Instead of personal trays they are using boards as serving trays with several mugs on each. Behind a reconstructed Birkenau barrack two girls are building a snowman. It is freezing. Several of the actors playing German SS guards are wearing large overcoats. They put them around the children to keep them warm. Spielberg rounds up several young girls and wants to rehearse a scene in which they are frightened and are calling for their mothers. Nothing doing—all the faces are smiling when they are yelling, "Mama! Save me! Help!" Dagmara, who is an interpreter for the extras, tells the children to think of something scary, like meeting a wolf in the forest. The children cannot believe that in Spielberg's film things could be scary.

Filming in Birkenau lasted two days and one night. When I drove there a week later with a film crew from Universal Pictures, the only company to whom Spielberg gave permission to make a documentary about the making of *Schindler's List*, the camp set was already dismantled without a trace. At the crematorium ruins in Birkenau I saw Miri Fabian (Mrs. Dresner) and Adi Nitzan (Mila Pfefferberg), who came there to see the camp. They had not wanted to visit it during filming.

The Płaszów concentration camp where most of the scenes would take place was reconstructed in the Liban quarry. At the turn of the century the quarry was named after a Kraków businessman, Bernard Liban, who owned a Portland cement factory in nearby Bonarka and a soda factory in Borek Fałęcki, two communities near Kraków. The soda factory was later bought by a Belgian concern owned by Ernest Solvay.

The Liban quarry has a war history of its own. On April 15, 1942, the Germans established a penal camp for construction workers in the quarry; Der Straflager des Baudienstes im Generalgouvernement [The Prison Camp for Construction Workers in the General Gubernia]. Most just used the short name, S-Lager Kraków, or just Liban. After the start of the Russian offensive in July 1944, there was a panic among the guards and prisoners at Liban. On July 21, 1944, most of them escaped, except for twenty-three prisoners. When the panic was over and the guards had returned, Beneke, the commandant of Liban, ordered all remaining prisoners locked up in one of the barracks. Later he let them go, telling them to escape. It was a trick. As they were running away, he ordered the guards to shoot at them. Nearly all perished.

There were only three barracks in the original camp in Liban. Now, on the bottom of the quarry, thirty-four barracks have been constructed at a cost of $600,000. Everything was built out of nice lumber—six hundred cubic meters of smooth finished boards shining in the morning sun. On the crown of the quarry and surrounding the camp are eleven watchtowers. At the gate someone put up a tablet with a sign in Polish: "Attention! Camp Area! STOP! Photography Forbidden! Trespassers will be shot without warning!" Some took photos anyway.

The first days of filming in Liban are devoted to scenes of the building of the Płaszów camp by Jewish prisoners. About four hundred extras, men and women, participate. Some portray the Ukrainian guards at the gate, others are building the barracks. I notice redheaded Agnieszka, a student of archeology at Jagiellonian University. She is carrying boards and beams. This is really hard physical work. Penetrating wind blows from the east. It is cold, though we are somewhat protected by the walls of the quarry. Steven Spielberg's assistants, Sergio Mimica-Gezzan and Marek Brodzki, are preparing the next setup. All the extras have something to do, even those who are not in the view of the cameras. One never knows what shots the director will want to take.

Marek Brodzki began his several years adventure in film with Zbigniew Kuźmiński's serial, *Ostrowska Republic*. Later there were collaborations with Jerzy Sztwiertnia, Andrzej Domalik, Marek Koterski, and Janusz Majewski. He has also worked as a collaborator or assistant with several renowned directors such as John Irving, Pilar Miro, and [Constantine] Costa-Gavras [director of the famous 1969 Oscar-winning film *Z*]. Most often, however, he assisted Krzysztof Zanussie in films such as *Wherever You Are* (Poland, 1988), *Inventory* (Poland, 1989), *Life for Life* (Poland, 1991), and *The Silent Touch* (Poland, 1990), with Max von Sydow. Marek has a booming voice—a necessary attribute for an assistant director. On location we joke that when Marek yells, "ACTION!" *against* the wind, one can hear him as far as the Bell of Zygmunt in the Wawel belfry; and *with* the wind—even further.*

I hide behind a barrack wall and find a thick straw doormat to stand on because the frost is biting my toes. Now it is warmer. David James, the official still photographer for *Schindler's List*, walks up to me. He leaves some of his equipment in my care. The batteries in his equipment gave out after taking fewer than twenty pictures. His hands are freezing. The gloves he wears are rather thin in order to facilitate handling his photographic equipment. David blows into his hands and then installs new batteries. On the set he must be in the front line all the time, right next to the director and the camera.

---

*The Zygmunt Bell is a giant bell cast in 1520 by Hans Beham. It was paid for by King Zigmunt I the Old, and hung at the top, or third, level in Wawel's Castle Cathedral belfry. The largest bell in Poland, it weighs 11 tons, is 2.6 meters in diameter, and 2 meters high. Requiring fully twelve men to ring it, it is rung only four times a year—on special national and church holidays.

Steven Spielberg is setting up a scene in which Amon Goeth, the commander of the Płaszów camp from 1943 to 1944, is selecting a maid for his villa. During a cold day like today everyone would like to get work inside the protection of four walls, even if it means to work for Amon Goeth—as long as one does not have to carry heavy beams and could warm up a bit. Wearing white gloves, Amon Goeth walks along a row of young women standing in the cold. He chooses the one who did not volunteer for the job. This really happened, just as everything else in this film. The mythological Amon, the chief god in the Egyptian pantheon, could give life or take it away—and Amon Goeth most often took it away. I witnessed a discussion among some German actors playing in *Schindler's List* who were born after the war, so they really did not carry a guilt complex because of it. Still, they searched for an argument that Amon Goeth could not have been born a real German. "Amon! What kind of name is that?" they said. "What real German would have such a name?"

Ralph Fiennes, a British actor, portrays Amon Goeth. His last film was a new version of Emily Jane Brontë's *Wuthering Heights* (1992). He also played Lawrence in a made-for-television film, *A Dangerous Man: Lawrence After Arabia* (1990)* but British theatergoers value him in Shakespearean tragic roles most of all. Now he portrays a particularly cruel and hated figure. Spielberg chose an actor with good looks and a charming smile. Amon Goeth's maid, Helen Hirsch, remembers him as a cruel beast. The director does not want Amon Goeth to be drawn

---

*Ralph Fiennes has become quite well-known to American audiences since making *Schindler's List* and his Academy Award nomination as Best Supporting Actor of 1993. Though he did not receive the Oscar (it went to Tommy Lee Jones for *The Fugitive*), he did receive the Best Supporting Actor Award from the British Academy of Film and Television for his portrayal of Amon Goeth. His films since include *Quiz Show* (1994), *Strange Days* (1995), *The English Patient* (1996), which received an Oscar for Best Picture and the nomination of Fiennes for Best Actor, *Oscar and Lucinda* (1997), and *The Avengers* (1997).

with a black-and-white line—a cartoon. He has to be more complicated. His likable appearance should be in contrast to his dark soul.

Ralph has piercing steel eyes. I witnessed his conversation with a woman who was in the Płaszów camp and knew the real Amon Goeth. Ralph was interested in the behavior of the character he portrayed. Did Amon react violently? Did he scream? No, he did not scream or wave his arms; he moved as if in slow motion, but he aroused terror just by looking at a person. Ralph has that kind of look.

Suddenly the woman talking to him shudders as Ralph looks at her. Maybe there is some tragic memory. She says goodbye quickly and turns to leave. "But I am only an actor," Ralph tries to add, a note of sorrow in his gentle voice. He was himself again—Ralph Fiennes; the steel look in his eyes had softened.

The day before filming began, Lew Rywin asked me to represent the producers of the film and meet with a group of high school students from Israel. The young people had arrived in Kraków to spend a week getting acquainted with the place from which their parents and relatives had come and to pay tribute to the victims of the Holocaust—a one-week lesson in living history. In the morning they visited Płaszów, where they were told about Oskar Schindler. We met in a lecture hall. My job was to acquaint them with the creation of Keneally's book and Steven Spielberg's film. When we were finished and I was getting my coat from the cloak room, an older lady whom I had noticed sitting in the last row during the lecture walked up to me. She spoke Polish beautifully, and said, "You know I did not come with this group of young people. I joined your lecture to hear what you had to say about Płaszów. I was in that camp. My father, Zygmunt Grünberg, built the camp. He was a prominent architect in Kraków."

That's how I met Ziuta Grünberg, and she told me her story. I had already read about her in Stella Müller-Madej's book *Through a Child's Eyes*. Amon Goeth ordered her father to build a guardhouse for the SS men and set an unrealistic deadline. He locked up Ziuta and her mother in a prison bunker as hostages, threatening them with execution if the deadline wasn't met. Thanks to the incredible efforts of the workers, the building was finished on time and Ziuta and her mother were released from the death cell. Ziuta stayed in Płaszów and participated in the dismantling of the camp so that no trace would be left. Three days before the liberation of Kraków by the Red Army, Ziuta was evacuated to Auschwitz, where eventually she was liberated. Mr. Grünberg does not figure in the film. There is a woman architect, however, who registered a protest with Amon Goeth against building faulty foundations for the barracks. Amon Goeth ordered her shot. After she was dead, he admitted she was right.

With this scene Steven Spielberg ended the first stage of filming in Liban—the portion having to do with building the camp in winter. In the spring we would return for a couple of weeks.

On Saturday, March 6, the end of the first week of filming, Steven Spielberg and the producers wrote a letter to all who were working on the film:

Schindler's List

TO: Everybody
FROM: Steven Spielberg, Jerry Molen, Branko Lustig

We have come through very hard days together. We appreciate your effort, good will, and enthusiasm. We have been working under extremely difficult conditions but this effort has not been in vain. We are deeply convinced that we will make a wonderful, significant picture, which will spread our message of peace all over the world.

Yours very gratefully,

Steven Spielberg
Jerry Molen
Branko Lustig

It was then that Steve Zaillian, the scriptwriter for *Schindler's List*, arrived in Kraków. The initial version of the script numbered 130 pages. After Spielberg's alterations, the script had grown to 190 pages, but the number of repeatedly rewritten pages surpassed the number of the pages of the original script many times over, mainly because the dialogue on some of them was revised several times. Typically, each consecutive change in the script is printed on pages of a different color. At the end of filming, the script usually looks like a rainbow and there are a very few pages of the original white color. By the end of the first week of filming for *Schindler's List*, the seventh consecutive set of changes had been printed—on green paper.

6

The Road to the Ghetto

Saturday, March 27, 1993. The schedule calls for the filming of three scenes that took place inside the *Judenrat*—Jewish Senior Council—headquarters in the fall of 1939. The Jews discuss the orders from the German occupation authorities. Here Schindler meets Itzhak Stern for the first time. He will consult Itzhak, a former bookkeeper for the Record Emalia factory on Zabłocie, on whether it is worth it to buy into that business. For the actors playing that scene it meant the workday began at 6:15 A.M. The setting was the interior of an old building on the corner of Krakówska and Skawińska Streets, next to the former Jewish hospital.

Let's recall some of the historical events of 1939:

> September 17: A Jewish municipality is formed on the order of German occupation authorities.
> September 27: The chief of the first operational group of the secret police, B. Streckenbach, is ordered to organize a Jewish senior council—the *Judenrat*—and complete a census of the Jewish population. Result: there are 68,482 Jews living in Kraków.

October 10: Jews receive district identity cards [*Kennkarte*] with a yellow stripe.

October 26: Compulsory work is ordered. All Polish people from the ages of eighteen to sixty have to work; Jews from the age of twelve to sixty. Jews are forbidden to practice kosher methods for the slaughter of cattle and poultry.

October 30: Himmler, as commissioner in charge of strengthening German purification, orders the transportation of Jews from annexed territories to the General Gubernia, formerly Poland.

November 23: All Jewish stores are ordered to display a Star of David.

November 24: Use of the Hebrew language is forbidden.

November 27: All Jews are ordered to surrender their automobiles and motorcycles.

December 1: From this day forth all Jews age twelve and over are ordered to wear white armbands with a blue Star of David.

December 6: All Jews are ordered to surrender gold, silver, and any currency, except for 2,000 złoty (the unit of Polish currency).

December 13: All Jewish schools are ordered closed; Jewish students and teachers are removed from other schools.

So much for the historical background.

In the scene to be filmed of the Kraków *Judenrat,* the Jews conclude that it cannot get any worse. After all, there are international agreements which mandate that the convictions of others be respected; there are human rights. The future showed that it *could* be worse. On April 12, 1940, at a meeting of the Office of the General Gubernia, it was decided to move all the Jews out of Kraków, except for ten thousand skilled workers. By June 1, 1940, the number of Jews in Kraków diminished from sixty-eight thousand to fifty-four thousand because of the move. An additional thirty-three thousand were moved out during August 1940.

In connection with these resettlements, as they were called, Poldek Page-Pfefferberg told me another of his unbelievable-but-true stories. Before the war, Poldek was an instructor for the Polish Association of Skiers. During preparations for a competition in 1939, Sepp Roehr, a German skier and instructor, arrived in Zakopane to join with Polish skiers and film a commercial advertising this Tatra Mountain resort. Poldek participated in that venture because he was a good skier and spoke German. After the outbreak of the war, it became clear that Sepp Roehr was a German spy. In Zakopane he became known for his audacity in arresting, among others, his former skiing partners and competitors—Bronek Czech and the famous Marusarz brothers—apparently only because they had been his rivals in numerous skiing competitions.

During the resettlement of Jews from Kraków, Poldek and his family were ordered to leave the city. Poldek decided to try to secure a change in the decision by appealing to a German city official, but the official was not available. Poldek was directed to the assistant who, to Poldek's surprise, was Sepp Roehr. He, too, was no less surprised when Poldek told him that he was Jewish and had received orders to leave Kraków.

"You had to do something really bad," said Roehr, "that they didn't let you stay in town."

"Only," Poldek answered, "that as a Polish officer I fought against you and you as a German officer fought against me."

"I'll see what I can do for you," Sepp Roehr answered.

He really did—he pulled Poldek and his wife Mila from an assembly point in an old Austrian fort on Mogilska Street, from which Jews were being transported to concentration camps. Poldek's parents, however, could not be saved. They were deported and perished.

On March 3, 1941, the chief of the Kraków district gave

orders to form a ghetto in Podgórze, a suburb of Kraków.
March 20 was the deadline for all Jews who had a permit to
reside in Kraków to move into the ghetto, which was surrounded by a wall and barbed wire. About twelve thousand Jews
moved. They crossed the Wisła River on two bridges, one at the
end of Starowiślna Street and the other one at the end of
Krakówska Street. Today only the latter remains as it was then.

Today is Saturday afternoon, March 27, 1993. According to the
script it is March 20, 1941, the last day of the Jewish exodus to
the ghetto. The scene will involve about eight hundred extras in
addition to the individual actors who play the Pfefferbergs
(Poldek and Mila) and others. There are fifteen horse-drawn
wagons, pushcarts, birds in cages, cats, dogs, chickens; everything is ready at 10:00 A.M. Alpine climbers removed TV
antennas from the roofs of houses that would be in the view of
cameras. The first take of marching Jews is filmed on Try-
nitarska Street, next to the Bonifratry Hospital. Spielberg is
satisfied with just one rehearsal and orders actual filming. One
camera is placed on the sidewalk, another one on a boom to film
from above.

They are going. Some in fox furs, others in coats threadbare
to the wind. The poor and the rich. The remnants of the
thousands of Kraków Jews whose ancestors lived there for seven
centuries, contributing to the culture of Poland. They march in
front of the cameras for about two minutes—eight hundred of
them. The director will probably use less than half of the film
shot. After that one take he has enough material and does not
have to repeat it. Then we are moving to set up for the scene on
the bridge.

There are German documentary films of that exodus. In
those films a few Jews walk over the bridge, some ride in horse-
drawn wagons, someone pushes a cart. In my mind's eye there
remains the vivid image of an old Jew with a gray beard. The

photographer captured him after he had already crossed the bridge: The old Jew stops for a moment as if pondering the fate of the Eternal Wandering Jew.

There are no great crowds in those German documentaries. Spielberg, though, wants to have a lot of people in the scene. It is better to have the frame of the camera image filled. There is also another change from the original march: the direction is reversed from that of fifty-two years ago. In the film the Jews are leaving Podgórze instead of going to it. The reason for that change was to avoid burdening the regular population with transportation problems. If the direction had been the other way, the traffic on Krakówska Street and the bridge would have had to stop, especially the streetcars. The way it was filmed, the streetcars could turn, bypass the bridge, and cross the river on the next bridge. If the action had been filmed with historical accuracy, a large part of Podgórze would have had to be cut off for most of the day. With this minor "reversal" of history only a small detour was required for the locals.

In the documentaries, the Polish people watching this tragic march years ago are seen reacting in a variety of ways. Some watch the proceedings in silence, terrified with premonitions. Are they thinking that after the Jews it will be the Polish people? Others yell, "Jews be gone! We do not want you here! Go back where you came from!" As if those wretched ones had a place to return to. There are some who throw mud at those passing by.*

In Thomas Keneally's book and in the script based on it, this is the only scene in which Polish people are featured as a entity, a group. In all the other scenes in the book there are only

---

*There is a reason for the negative attitude on the part of some Polish people toward the Jews moving to the ghetto. The Germans created the ghetto by displacing all the Polish people who lived in the part of town chosen for the ghetto, so the process of resettling the Jews to ghettos brought about resettlement problems for many Polish families as well. The displaced Poles resented it bitterly, but though their lives had been disrupted, they were not made prisoners or victims of the Nazis' "Jewish problem," as were the Jews themselves.

Germans and Jews. Some critics formulated the thesis that the
book was anti-Polish. On the other hand, I agree with those who
do not consider the absence of Polish people anti-Polish—and
the scenes of throwing mud at the Jews? Could it have happened? Who can say with a clear conscience that it did not? I
read two scripts for *Schindler's List*, by two different writers. In
both, the mud-throwing scenes were included.

Ben Kingsley stops on the sidewalk next to the marching
crowd. He is not in his costume and has no makeup. He is upset
because of an incident that happened a short time ago back at
the hotel. An older man walked up to one of the Israeli actors
and asked him if he was Jewish. The actor confirmed it. Then
the intruder made a gesture of cutting one's throat and hanging. There could have been a fistfight if Kingsley had not
intervened. There were a few similar occurrences that were
interpreted as anti-Semitic, and everybody is very sensitive to it.

Elżbieta Szlufik, from the Interdepartmental Institute of History and Culture of Polish Jews at Jagiellonian University and
the author of the introduction to the then unpublished Polish
translation of *Schindler's List*, talked about the march of the
Kraków Jews to the ghetto on a broadcast by Radio Kraków in
1990. To our shame, she stated that historical testimonies
reaffirm the offensive behavior of Polish people against the
Jews. Was this representative of a majority of the Polish people?
I am certain it was not. Those who yell and behave aggressively
are always more visible than those who live and act in silence.

A story with which I became familiar two years ago may add
to the understanding of the varied behavior of human beings.
The incident occurred during the exodus of the Kraków Jews to
the Podgórze ghetto. Its participants lived in the back of a
house to the right of the exodus route. It is possible that they
stood on the sidewalk and watched the Jews passing, so I think it
is fitting to include the account here.

I was told the story on a warm evening in August as the crickets chirped in the trees of the park surrounding the old Konopki Mansion in Modlnica [an area near Kraków]. The mansion serves as a home for some of Jagiellonian University's creative workshops. The occasion was the ceremony marking the conclusion of the first summer institute devoted to a study of the history and fate of the Kraków Jews. The seminars were organized by the university's Interdepartmental Institute of History and Culture of the Polish Jews. The diplomas had been given out, and it was during the reception that one of the participants walked up to me. Judging from his age, he had not come here to learn but rather to search for his roots. I was not mistaken. He was Bernard O., from California. After a short introduction, I told him about my profession.

"I was born in Kraków," he said. "I came here for remembrance and also to find a Polish family who gave me shelter and a hiding place for one night. They saved my life. Though it was only one night, I remember their name and address. Now, almost half a century after that incident, I went to that house but no one by the name of Szewczyk—that was the name of the Polish family who saved me—lived there any more, and no one knew what happened to them, whether they survived the war or perished. The present tenants moved in after the war, but I would like to find the people who gave a twelve-year-old Jew one night's shelter, taking a chance with their lives while giving him the gift of life."

I did not have to pry long to get Bernard to tell me his entire story: "I was eight years old when the war started. For almost forty years I did not look back into my past, but other Jews who survived the Holocaust convinced me that I do not have the right to be silent about my experiences.

"I lived in Podgórze on Krakus Street. My parents had a small store; they sold cigarettes, tobacco, and newspapers. Frequently, we played hide-and-seek in the Krzemionki hills and in the park. There were a lot of places for hiding. I did not know that some day the game of hide-and-seek would be a game for my

life. We had a very modest apartment. I remember a sideboard
with dishes, separate for meat and separate for dairy products,
and a bottle of vodka from which my father poured himself a
small glass for special occasions. I remember a box for potatoes
and an oil lamp. We brought water from a well in our backyard.
I still remember the aroma of meat soup with noodles. My
uncle, Jósef Markowicz, lived with his wife and two sons around
the corner. I went there every week to the *mikveh* [a ritual bath]
and to the synagogue. Everybody around was a relative or a
friend. When I went to *cheder* [a Jewish school for boys], I passed
by a prison on Czarnecki Street. It is the only thing that has not
changed since my childhood. All that is left of the Old Synagogue on Węgierska Street are the walls and remnants of a
roof, with a birch tree growing on top of it.

"We lived near the border of the ghetto. I was busy, as were
many of my friends, smuggling food to the ghetto. Everyone
suffered great hunger. While I was outside the ghetto during
one of my expeditions for food, my mother happened to be
standing in line for bread. A German soldier sicked a dog on
her. My brother told me about it thirty years later. He could not
talk about it sooner.

"My father and I worked in the ghetto repairing shoes. My
two older brothers Salomon and Natan were prisoners in the
camp in Wieliczka.* The Germans kept reducing the size of the
ghetto and the number of Jews permitted to live there. They

---

*Wieliczka is a town located about twelve miles from Kraków and
famous since medieval times for its extraordinary salt mine. Containing a complex network of tunnels, rooms, and shafts within its
nine levels, the mine has drawn centuries of the famous and ordinary
to visit its remarkable corridors and view some large old chambers
which the miners have fashioned into awesome cathedral-like spaces
rich with carvings, sculpture, and natural wonders. During the war
the Germans set off a part of the town as a concentration camp. They
used the mine as a manufacturing facility for arms, utilizing Jewish
slave laborers. The mine was valued by the Germans for its natural
bombproof character.

transported them to concentration camps. My mother and sister were taken away while I was not home—I had gone on one of my 'trips' to get food on the outside.

"When the Kraków ghetto was liquidated, I was taken with my father to the camp in Płaszów. Almost every day a group of prisoners was lead towards a hill on top of which was an old military fort. We heard shots. I was twelve years old and I was curious to know what was on the other side of the hill, so I sneaked up there. I saw heaps of bodies. Then one day the Germans rounded up all the children in Płaszów, including myself. We were loaded onto a horse-drawn wagon. I was sure we were being taken to be shot. I was able to jump out of the wagon and hide in the Krzemionki hills, waiting till dark. At night I went onto Kalwaryjska Street, where the Polish family of my playmate lived in the back part of the house. They gave me shelter for that one night. Subsequently I found my uncle, with whom I went into hiding in the now vacant ghetto, but that one night remained the most important. ·

"For some time I continued to hide in the ghetto, where about fifty Jews were still cleaning up. When they finished their job, they were taken to the camp in Płaszów and executed. I was smuggled back to Płaszów to join my father, Jakub. The Płaszów camp was being liquidated and the prisoners taken to Auschwitz. One day our turn came and my father and I were taken to Birkenau. The thirty-mile trip lasted three days and three nights, and then there was a selection. I was sent to one side—the life side, my father to the other—the gas chamber and crematorium side. After we had been separated, we looked at each other from a distance. I was sure that we would not see each other again, but I was alive and I believed that God must have saved me.

"When the Russian soldiers were approaching, I was evacuated from Birkenau, taken deeper into German territory, and finally put in a concentration camp near Munich. That's where I was liberated. An American tanker outfit adopted me—they treated me like I was their mascot. After three months I returned to Kraków. Six more months of searching and I found my two older brothers, whose fate had been unknown to me all that time. It turned out that they, too, went through Birkenau.

"This is my story of the Holocaust," said Bernard.

There was still the matter of the Szewczyk family, who gave Bernard shelter for that one fateful night. I wanted to help him find them somehow. We decided to meet the next day on Kalwaryjska Street. In the courtyard of the house where Bernard found shelter, we made a videotape asking for information and possible contact. It was broadcast the same day, just before midnight on the national Polish Television news. Early next morning I was awakened by a telephone call from Tarnow. It was Mr. Szewczyk's son. His father was not alive. He had died several years ago in America.

I am standing on the sidewalk with Jurek Armata, a newspaper man from *Gazeta Wyborcza* who was invited by Lew Rywin to the film location. Branko Lustig joins us and asks my opinion about the scene just filmed. My answer is that if the Polish people figure prominently only in the scene we just witnessed, then *Schindler's List* destroys one stereotype—a good German is a dead German—as it reinforces another—the anti-Semitic Pole. Destroying one stereotype by replacing it with another is not the best way to achieve the truth.

The scene which we had just watched depicts a little girl standing in a crowd of Polish people watching the exodus march of the Jews. The girl looks at Olek Rosner, her playmate, going to the ghetto with his parents, and says, "Goodbye." Does she mean, "Till we see each other," or does she mean, "Farewell"? One is hopeful, the other quite the opposite. How will it play in Spielberg's film? Or maybe the take will end on the cutting-room floor altogether.

We break for lunch. A prop man standing by some properties places a dark cloth over a birdcage with a canary. It has cooled off considerably—to just 34°F. Snowflakes drift down from time to time. Will the canary survive this day's filming of the exodus?

Tomorrow's schedule calls for the filming of the ghetto liquidation as Oskar Schindler and his girl friend Ingrid observe it from the hill called Krzemionki. Again the flow of traffic will be changed for busses and streetcars. On Lwowska Street hundreds of TV antennas have been removed from the roofs. The residents are assured they will be remounted in two days, but heavy snow falls overnight. Branko Lustig wakes up with a funny feeling at 2:00 A.M. and looks out of the window. Everything is white and more is coming down. The telephones start to ring—to Lew Rywin, other producers. A decision has to be made—what to do? Of course the simplest thing is to call off the filming, but that would mean a loss of one production day. Finally, it is decided that a few interior scenes will be filmed and the open-air scenes will take place next Sunday. The scene designers and dressers go to work in the middle of the night. In a few hours, they construct "offices" and Oskar Schindler's Brinnlitz apartment in old storerooms at the Liban quarry. The actors are notified of the changes in schedule.

When Spielberg arrives on the location, he says, "These are not the scenes I prepared." Everything is organized with such precision, however, that the day is not wasted. The only difference—this Sunday he works just nine hours instead of twelve.

7

Putting It All Together:
About Directors, Actors, Producers,
and the Legitimacy of Our Hero

Before *Schindler's List*, I had never closely observed the process of making a film, but like anyone with an interest, I had a preconceived idea about filming that had developed only from seeing many films. According to that stereotype a director sits next to the camera on a chair with a sign, "Director." When I try to recall such a stereotype, most often in my mind's eye I see Hitchcock sitting in that chair. A friend of mine who knows about such things told me that Hitchcock prepared the script so thoroughly that on the set all the directorial responsibility was given to his assistant. He himself sat quietly in his chair.

If this was really true, then Spielberg is in absolute contrast to Hitchcock. Of course, on the set for *Schindler's List* there are several chairs: the usual wooden, folding "director's" chairs with deep blue canvas. The "owner's" name is embroidered in white. When they are lined up in the order of hierarchy, one can read: "Steven Spielberg"; then the producers: "Jerry Molen," "Branko Lustig," "Lew Rywin"; and the cinematographer: "Janusz Kamiński." Then come the two main actors: "Liam Neeson" and "Ben Kingsley"—playing Oskar Schindler and Itzhak Stern,

(*Left*) Second Lieutenant Leopold Page (Poldek Pfefferberg). Photographed at the time he was commissioned, November 11, 1938. (© Leopold Page)

(*Below*) Oskar Schindler, probably 1943. (© Leopold Page)

Oskar Schindler with his horse in the camp he built at the Brinnlitz factory, 1944–45.
(© Leopold Page)

Jews being made to clean away the snow on Szewska Street, Kraków, January 1940. A similar event from January 1941 is recreated in the film. (Collection of the State Archive of Kraków.)

Oskar Schindler, 1944, wearing the Tyrolean hat for which he had become famous. He wore this hat at the Brinnlitz station when he greeted the train that brought the 298 women rescued from Auschwitz. (© Leopold Page)

(*Right*) One of the Chassidic Kraków Jews photographed during the move to the ghetto. (Collection of the State Archive of Kraków)

(*Below*) Jews in Kraków being loaded onto freight cars for transport to concentration camps. (Collection of the State Archive of Kraków)

German officers checking the papers of a Jewish couple on their way to the ghetto. (Collection of the State Archive of Kraków)

Jews moving to the ghetto across the "Third Bridge," March 1941. A similar event is recreated in the film. (Collection of the State Archive of Kraków)

Machine gun installed over the Płaszów camp. (Collection of the translators)

Personnel at the Płaszów camp, 1943–45. This is the type of photo-album snapshot the serviceman of the period took to send home to his mother or girlfriend. (Collection of the translators)

Another snapshot of the personnel at the Płaszów camp, 1943–45. These soldiers appear to have been roaming in the fields gathering flowers. (Collection of the translators)

Snapshot of a German guard at the Płaszów camp in an off-duty moment with his trained guard dog, 1943–45. (Collection of the translators)

Women laborers pulling large ore cars (three in tandem, filled with stones) uphill in the Płaszów camp. (© Leopold Page)

Amon Goeth sleeping on a lawn chair at his villa, Płaszów Camp, 1943–44. (© Leopold Page)

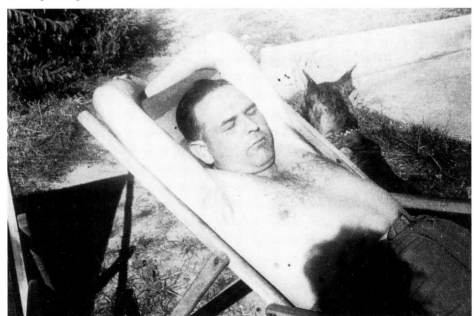

Amon Goeth on the balcony of his villa overlooking Płaszów camp.
(© Leopold Page)

Men in the Płaszów camp pushing ore cars filled with stones.
(© Leopold Page)

Oskar Schindler's secretaries photographed in front of the Emalia factory, 1944. Victoria Klonowska is fourth from the left. (© Leopold Page)

Fourth anniversary of the Emalia factory. Schindler, *center,* with "his" Jews. A similar event is recreated in the film. (© Leopold Page)

Oskar Schindler, *second from right,* Munich, April 1946, with some of the Jews he saved. *Standing, left to right:* Manci Rosner, Mundek Horowitz, Ludmila Page, Oskar Schindler, Rose Kippel. *Seated, left to right:* Halinka Horowitz, Olek Rosner, Pesia Bloch. (© Leopold Page)

(*Right*) Amon Goeth in the witness box at his trial, Kraków, 1945. (Collection of the translators)

(*Above*) Oskar Schindler, *seated,* and Leopold Page, Paris, November 1963. (© Leopold Page)

(*Left*) Leopold Page and Franciszek Palowski at the site of the original Płaszów camp near Krakow during the filming of an interview for Polish television in August 1985. (© Jerzy Druzkowski)

Marjacki Bazylika (St. Mary's Basilica) on the corner of Rynek Główny (the town square) in Kraków. (© Leopold Page)

(*Above*) Steven Spielberg at the Auschwitz-Birkenau camp, January 1992. (Collection of the author)

(*Inset*) A portion of the Płaszów camp set constructed for the film. (Collection of the author)

(*Left*) Leopold Page, Ludmila Page, and Franciszek Palowski. The Płaszów camp set is in the background. (© Leopold Page)

The author and friends during filming at the Kamienna Street train station. (Collection of the author)

Steven Spielberg, Ryszard and Anna Horowitz, and Ryszard's sister, Niusia Karakulska, Jerusalem, May 1993. As children, Ryszard and Niusia were on Schindler's original list. (Collection of the author)

Preparing for filming at the Catholic Cemetery in Jerusalem, May 1993. (Collection of the author)

Steven Spielberg documenting his first visit to Kraków with a video camera, January 1992, at the Remuh synagogue. (© Marek Brokzki)

Steven Spielberg in the Podgórze district at one of two remaining original ghetto walls during his first visit to Kraków, 1992. *Left to right:* Scriptwriter Steven Zaillian, the author, *back to camera,* and Steven Spielberg. (© Marek Brokzki)

(*Above*) The Amon Goeth villa as reconstructed for the film, seen from the Płaszów camp side. (© Leopold Page)

(*Inset*) The original Amon Goeth villa at the Płaszów camp as seen from the street. (Collection of the translators)

(*Left*) Steven Spielberg on the Płaszów Camp set. (© Ryszard Kornecki)

Liam Neeson (Oskar Schindler) and Beatrice Macola (as Schindler's girlfriend Ingrid) doing a take for the sequence filmed on Krzemionki Hill in which Schindler observed the liquidation of the ghetto and sees the little girl, Genia, in the red coat, April 4, 1993 (see cover photo). (© Leopold Page)

In the old Jewish section of Kraków called Kazimierz. Preparing to film a sequence on Szeroka Street, waiting for the action to begin. (© Leopold Page)

Filming a scene on Szeroka Street. (© Leopold Page)

Leopold Page (Poldek Pfefferberg, *center*) on the Szeroka Street set, surrounded by actors: *second from the left,* Ben Kingsley; *second from the right,* Ralph Fiennes. (© Leopold Page)

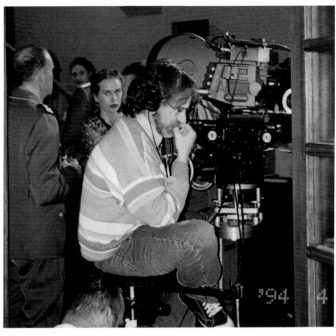

During filming of the poker game between Amon Goeth and Oskar Schindler that is to decide the fate of Helen Hirsch. Steven Spielberg next to his camera contemplating "how to do it."
(© Leopold Page)

Filming the making of the souvenir photo celebrating the opening of the Emalia factory.
(© Leopold Page)

Piotr Polk and Jacek Wójcicki as the brothers Rosner. (© Leopold Page)

Leopold Page (Poldek Pfefferberg) and Ludmila Page giving Steven Spielberg a painting by Pawel Vogler. (© Leopold Page)

The Order of the Smile ceremony. Steven Spielberg, *center,* talking with the children, with E.T., *above,* and the Kraków (Wawel) Dragon, *right, rear.* (© Ryszard Kornecki)

Steven Spielberg with three generations of "Schindler Jews." *Right to left:* Niusia Karakulska, her daughter, and her grandson. Photographed on the Płaszów camp set. (Collection of the author)

Leopold Page with Steven Spielberg discussing the filming of the scene in the Catholic Cemetery, Jerusalem, May 1993. (© Leopold Page)

Oskar Schindler's grave in the Catholic Cemetery, Jerusalem. (© Leopold Page)

respectively. There are also chairs simply marked "Actor." Only a few "owners" of their chairs would ever sit on them during filming.

One day I was invited onto the set by one of the producers and had an opportunity to sit briefly in Liam Neeson's chair, but the first time I saw Steven Spielberg in his chair was the fifteenth day of filming—about the middle of the third week of work. He sat down to concentrate and ponder before the next scene. This happened during filming in the officers' casino where the nightclub scenes in Kraków during the war were shot. The sight of Spielberg sitting down in his chair surprised everyone—most of all his producers.

Most often Spielberg concentrates while pacing around. It doesn't bother him that he is surrounded by people swirling around like boiling water: the electricians setting up lights; the cameramen and their assistants mounting tracks for the cameras, changing lenses, loading cassettes with film. The Master is able to ignore all the feverish commotion and concentrate on the script. The *Schindler's List* script, in a cherry color binding with Spielberg's name on it, and a copy of Thomas Keneally's book are always within Spielberg's reach. During these moments of concentration between takes no one, not even the closest to him, dares to interrupt his solitude. There may be an exception, though, when the director of photography, Janusz Kamiński, has to consult on a specific problem of camera position.

Spielberg's favorite chair is behind the camera. His biographers emphasize that his favorite position is behind the camera, with one eye on the viewfinder. Frequently, I witnessed Spielberg filming an entire scene himself. The first time I saw this was a scene between Oskar Schindler and Amon Goeth in a small interior space—a short scene, forty or fifty seconds. It is near the end of the war. Amon Goeth has already been removed as commandant of the Płaszów camp, his career finished. He visits Schindler in Brinnlitz, where 1,200 Jews work for Schindler—the same Jews over whom in earlier days Amon

Goeth had limitless power. Spielberg is pleased with each take of the scene. He compliments the actors: "Magnificent, perfect! Wonderful, marvelous! I love it!"

Then he says, "Let's do it again."

Tactfully, even delicately, he suggests certain gestures, or a change in facial expression—but not because it was not good. It really was "wonderful" and he "loved it," but he often wanted one more, or maybe several more [takes].

Liam Neeson was the hero in *Schindler's List*. He is Irish but for many years has worked in the United States. He has many credits; among them are *Leap of Faith* (1992), *Husbands and Wives* (1992), *Darkman* (1990), *Under Suspicion* (1992), *Shining Through* (1992), *The Good Mother* (1988), and *Ethan Frome* (1993).* Before coming to Kraków he was on Broadway in Eugene O'Neill's *Anna Christie*. Neeson is an excellent actor but is not considered a major star. Spielberg did not want a star for Schindler. He did not want "stardom" to overpower the character. Therefore it took a long time to select a suitable actor. There were all kinds of rumors: Kevin Costner—supposedly he wanted to do it for free. Then Mel Gibson was mentioned. There were Polish actors considered: Piotr Fronczewski and Andrzej Seweryn. Seweryn was even invited to Hollywood for a screen test. Liam Neeson also had a screen test. Of all the candidates, Liam was physically the most like Oskar Schindler. Maybe he was a bit thinner.

A half year went by. Liam had not heard Spielberg's decision, if he had made one. Of course, from hearsay he knew about Costner and Gibson, so he did not hold out any hopes. One day Spielberg, his wife Kate, and her mother went to the theater to see Neeson in *Anna Christie*. After the performance they went back stage. *Anna Christie* is a very emotional drama, and Kate's mother was quite moved. Liam Neeson was so pleased that he embraced her and kissed her on both cheeks. That gesture was

---

*Liam Neeson's recent film credits include *Nell* (1994), *Rob Roy* (1995), *Before and After* (1996), *Michael Collins* (1996), and *Les Misérables* (1997).

the deciding factor. Spielberg thought Oskar Schindler, too, would react like that. A week later Neeson received Spielberg's invitation to play the lead in the film.

Liam has other traits in common with Schindler: for one, a magnetic influence on women. (Everybody talked about his relationship with Natasha Richardson, who even flew into Kraków for a few days during filming and later became his wife.) Liam also has a natural low-timbre voice; for Schindler, the result of cigarettes and cognac. Liam, however, like a real Irishman, prefers dark Guiness beer—as the Kraków bartenders found out. Liam wanted to imitate Oskar Schindler's manner of speech. Spielberg found a tape from the sixties with Schindler's voice. Liam listened to it many times, practicing Schindler's sound [his voice patterns and pitch].

My friend Janina recalled that Oskar Schindler had a great sense of humor. This was his personal charm, especially when he talked to his coworkers. He never used German, but a laughable mixture of Polish and Czech. He mispronounced words, made the most out of fracturing conventional expressions, and used incorrect grammar. The result was very funny. One day Janina heard him speak French to a friend of his who came to Kraków from the German embassy in Turkey on some secret mission. (Janina suspected it had something to do with the botched effort to assassinate Hitler in July 1944.) Schindler's French was worse than his Polish-Czech mishmash. In the film, of course, Liam speaks perfect English.

Spielberg avoided using stars in his films for many years—he considered the film to be the star. In choosing an "Everyman" or "Everyday Regular Guy," he was suggesting to us that we can all accomplish extraordinary things, just like the heroes in his films. More recently he has abandoned that principle: In the *Indiana Jones* trilogy he used stars, like Harrison Ford and Sean Connery; in *Hook*, Dustin Hoffman, Robin Williams, and Julia Roberts; and for *Schindler's List* he chose Ben Kingsley for an important part. Though he is not the lead, Kingsley serves almost as an alter ego for the character of Schindler. Spielberg believes that Ben Kingsley's portrayals are so great he doesn't need much makeup. Kingsley received an Oscar for creating the part of Gandhi (in 1982). He was also nominated for an Oscar for the part of Meyer Lanski in *Bugsy* (1991). Other films of his are *Testimony* (1988), *Without a Clue* (1988), *Pascali's Island* (1988), *The Turtle Diary* (1985), *Betrayal* (1983), and *Sneakers* (1992).* Kingsley became acquainted with the Holocaust theme playing the part of Simon Wiesenthal, a famous headhunter of Hitler war criminals, in the television film *Murderers Among Us: The Simon Wiesenthal Story* (1989). At that time Kingsley spent many hours with the man whom he portrayed. Thus he was well prepared, intellectually, for a part in a film about events from World War II.

Audiences identify Kingsley with his greatest role— Gandhi—so it is natural that one could seek an analogy between the part of Gandhi and the part of Itzhak Stern in the present film. After a showing of *Gandhi* at the Young People's Academy of Film, a question was asked about the analogy. Kingsley answered that he was lucky to be a successful actor but he has found it is important for him to separate himself from the character he is to portray:

> "I approach it like an artist painting a portrait. Each time as the creator of a portrait, I tear myself away from the personality in the portrait. That's what happened in the case of Gandhi," he said. "Each task in acting, each role demands an individual, special approach. Just like a painter facing an empty canvas or a sculptor in front of a lump of clay or stone—it is clean, untouched. In creating a role, I concentrate on eliminating any preexisting perceptions or attitudes from my own personality. Even the smallest part of me cannot intrude into that portrait. I strive to create a new personality. I must remain neutral—

---

*Ben Kingsley's recent film credits include *Searching for Bobby Fischer* (1993), *Dave* (1993), *Death and the Maiden* (1994), *Species* (1995), and *The Assignment* (1997).

the act of creating must remain clean. My task is not to evaluate, to condemn, to love, or to hate that character. I build the portrait of the character honestly by separating myself from that person. It is up to the audience to evaluate that character. My work is finished then. It remains to wash my hands and say, 'Here it is—my work— I created it for you.'"

That's how Ben Kingsley spoke of his creative process.

Many of the people involved in Spielberg's film have known each other for years, even though they might have contacts with one another only off and on. Working in the film industry, they must perform a variety of tasks. As an example, take Miki Stanisiç from Zagreb, Croatia. For *Schindler's List* he is Branko Lustig's "right hand," responsible for some of the most difficult tasks as well as for the more mundane: He knows how to find a truck lost somewhere on the highway while transporting costumes. If necessary, he will also tactfully remind a wardrobe person that an actor's boots are not polished as they should be. In an outdoor scene when the director wanted to soften the picture by covering it with fog, Miki would personally operate the fogging equipment. He may also act; he played a bit part in *Fiddler on the Roof* (1971). Branko Lustig loves to act too, and had a small part in each of the films that he produced: *Fiddler on the Roof* (1971), *The Tin Drum* (1979), *Sophie's Choice* (1982), and the television miniseries *The Winds of War* (1983), among others. In *Schindler's List* he also has a small part. He plays the maître d' in a Kraków nightclub where Oskar Schindler entertained his influential friends from among the German city administrators. Schindler was able to save many lives while serving good drinks and surrounded by beautiful women. The interior of the Kraków Officers Club served as the wartime nightclub setting.

On the set, Branko showed up in an elegant tuxedo instead of the crew's usual "uniform"—jeans. While waiting for his cue he may have to attend to some duties as a producer, so then he would put on a round cap like the skipper of a fishing boat.

Wearing the cap he was a producer, without the cap, an actor.

His scene was repeated several times—each time it was "excellent" but "let's repeat it." One time Branko mixed up the word sequence in a sentence. Ossi Ragheb—a German actor and, for many years, a language consultant with knowledge of English, German, Italian, and Arabic—listened carefully to be sure the dialogue was correct. He did not agree with Branko's change in the word sequence, so the take had to be repeated. Another time the silence on the set was broken by a siren from an ambulance rushing to a medical academy clinic on Kopernik Street.

My attention was caught by a tall young man who appeared on the set only during preparations and then disappeared. He was dressed in jeans but also wore an elegant jacket, white shirt, and bow tie. His name was Peter Thurell, an American who had lived in Poland for three years. Peter hangs around the filmmaking industry working as a stand-in. In *Schindler's List* he stood in for Liam Neeson. Because he is the same height and stature as Neeson the lights could be adjusted on him for the best view of the actor in the setting. Some of the other actors also had stand-ins: Ben Kingsley, Ralph Fiennes, and Caroline Goodall, who played Schindler's wife Emilie. Using a stand-in permits the actor to have makeup corrected, concentrate on the upcoming scene, or simply rest—on a chair with his or her name.

During filming in the officers club, I witnessed one of the longest scenes in *Schindler's List*. Taken by a handheld camera, the scene started on the first floor with Schindler's entrance. He then proceeded up the stairs, stopped halfway up, and with a lighter, lit a cigarette for a beautiful young woman. He did it casually, paying no attention to her looks. He then moved among the joke-telling German officers who got out of his way, impressed by his nonchalant assurance. Finally, he was stopped by a head waiter who got a big tip and immediately found him a table, at which Liam sat down. Spielberg chose the longest possible path for Neeson, who must have walked many yards with the camera following him step-by-step.

For smoothness, long scenes are usually filmed by a camera installed on a dolly with rubber tires or on metal tracks, but this could not be done because of the steps on which part of the action took place. Thus a "steadycam" was employed by Ray, the cameraman. A "steadycam" mounts right on the camera-man's body and is based on the gyroscope principle used in military tanks to steady and steer the barrel of the gun. This permits an ideal or constant level to be preserved independent of the unevenness of the terrain. The camera behaves similarly when mounted on the "steadycam." In spite of rough move-ment by the operator or even tripping, the movement in the filmed picture is always smooth.

Spielberg could not personally shoot the scenes when the camera was mounted in this fashion. A professional camera weighs over thirty-five pounds, so even Ray, who next to Spielberg looks like a professional athlete, would hand the camera to his assistant to carry it back to the number one position after each rehearsal and the usual "Let's take it again." The assistant, Jimmie, is six-foot, six-inches tall and even more athletic looking than Ray. He either pulled the camera dolly or carried the camera, and seemed to have endless energy. After heavy work on the set he took a lunch break "resting" by playing soccer; after work, he put on in-line skates and unloaded his surplus energy gliding on the streets, usually Floriańska Street.

Steven likes to see what the camera sees. When he does the filming himself, he looks through the viewfinder, and if he does not stand behind the camera he watches the image the camera "sees" on a video monitor mounted to the side of the camera. In the case of a long moving shot such as the one in the officers club, neither of these options was possible. Today's technology, however, offered a solution. A wireless video monitor system was employed and a miniature video camera was installed next to the camera on the "steadycam." Thus, Steven could "follow" Ray, the cameraman, and direct his every step, telling him exactly what image to capture.

Spielberg wanted to make this a film that would impress the

audience as cinema verité. One day on location, when Director
of Photography Janusz Kamiński remarked that what they were
doing was not in accordance with proper filmmaking, Steven
countered, "Everything we have done till now in this film is not
in accord with 'proper filmmaking.'" Of course, he made
everybody on the set laugh.

During the filming of the long scene with Liam Neeson in the
officers club, I tried to count the number of cigarettes Batia
Grafka, a properties mistress, inserted in the cigarette case of
the beautiful woman on the stairs. Liam lit the woman's
cigarette as he moved up the stairs, and there had to be a fresh
one for each take. I had lost count by the time Spielberg said,
"We have a take!"

In the afternoon Andrzej Seweryn showed up on the set. He
played SS-Oberführer Julian Scherner, head of the SS and of the
police of the Kraków district from August 1941 until March 1944.
I have known Andrzej personally since last year's "European
Month of Culture" in Kraków. He arrived with Peter Brook for
the Polish premiere of the film *Mahabharata* (1989), in which
Andrzej was cast. He is a wonderful fellow who once helped us as
an interpreter when we suddenly found ourselves at a loss, which
was before he was called to Hollywood to screen-test for the part
of Schindler. Today on the set, he met his rival who won the part.
I asked him how he felt about it, and he answered, "After all, one
sometimes has to lose, even in poker." Though he did not play
Schindler he was still fascinated by this man and the motives for
his deeds. So many myths, legends, and—in some circles—
resentments grew up around Schindler's person.

Stanislaw Dobrowolski, leader of the Kraków division of the
underground organization Żegota,* wrote a book, *Memoirs of a*

*Żegota was an underground organization established in 1941
under primary financial support from the exile Polish government in

Pacifist. In this he asked many questions concerning Oskar Schindler, such as, "What purpose is served by the idea of whitewashing an agent of the Abwehr* and a war hyena born in Czechoslovakia?" He had three singular hypotheses: first, the whitewashing benefited a group of camp inmates who became "specially privileged" because they had been able to afford expensive presents for Schindler and his supervisors; after the war they wanted to mislead "international and Israeli opinion." The second Dobrowolski hypothesis: the need for a whitewash resulted from the meeting between Prime Minister David Ben Gurion and Chancellor Konrad Adenauer of Germany, in which it was decided that the German government would pay Israel restitution for the war victims. Both politicians needed an example of a "good German" for propaganda purposes. In the third hypothesis Dobrowolski suspected that perhaps something much more serious was at play, namely, "an attempt to discredit in world opinion the legitimacy and maybe even the legality of the Nuremberg trials, especially against the criminal bureaucrats." Dobrowolski sounded the alarm that "a director Page-Lesserberg had already contacted Kraków." Dobrowolski asked if that "director" intended to consult with Polish historians about those scenes which portray Polish people, before a movie about Schindler was made.

The alleged director was Poldek Page-Pfefferberg, who did not have to consult with Polish historians about anything because this was his own history—the history of a Polish Jew and a Polish army officer. Those Jewish "specially privileged camp

---

London. It was formed to assist Jews in getting passports, papers, etc., to escape the Holocaust. About thirty thousand Jews were helped in this manner.

*Schindler was working for the German Intelligence Service [Abwehr] in Czechoslovakia before he came to Kraków. Dobrowolski is referring to an undocumented claim some have made that because Schindler had been doing intelligence work for the Germans before coming to Kraków, he must have been spying also when he came to Kraków.

inmates," as Dobrowolski describes them, who were they? The
1,200 Schindler Jews who gave unanimous testimony con-
firming the stand Schindler took.

To conclude the point, it is worth quoting a fragment from
Maciej Kozłowski's mid-eighties polemic that appeared in *Tygod-
nik Powszechny*, which earlier had carried his review of Thomas
Keneally's book—the first review by the Polish press. He
responded to Dobrowolski that membership in a criminal
structure is not itself a criminal act. "As long as criminal and
even fundamentally bad and deceitful structures will exist, for
just as long the doubts and dilemmas which Oskar Schindler
faced will remain open challenges to human consciousness." It
is not a crime to "play the game"; it is a crime to violate the
fundamental conscience of humanity.

Poldek Page sent Stanislaw Dobrowolski's book to me from
Los Angeles while I was in New York. He enclosed his own
opinion, one that was decidedly less elegant than the retort by
Maciej Kozłowski and which I dare not quote, whereas I can
quote an elegantly succinct comment recalled from the end of
the documentary Jon Blair made for Thames Television. It was
made in 1983, soon after the appearance of Thomas Keneally's
book about Oskar Schindler. At the end of this film, which
received the highest recognition accorded a television show that
year—a kind of British Emmy—Ryszard Horowitz, the youn-
gest of the Schindler Jews, remarked: "I feel a certain homage
to the man, whoever he was and however he did it. Who cares?
Life is really what counts."

I think we are now at the terminus of this whole "Schindler
Affair." When I saw Ryszard Horowitz's sister, Niusia Karakulska, whom Schindler saved, her daughter, and her grandson on the set of Steven Spielberg's film, I understood that in
the face of this miracle—a miracle for three generations of
life—all academic considerations of the moral fundamentalists
are not only specious but also absolutely without merit.

Unfortunately our meeting with Andrzej Seweryn and the discussion about Schindler was interrupted by Sergio Mimica-Gezzan, second to Mark Brodzki, assistant to Steven Spielberg. He asked Andrzej to get ready because soon Steven would need him on the set for a scene with Liam Neeson.

An acquaintance of mine who had carefully observed the acting method of Polish actors in *Schindler's List* compared them with their foreign colleagues. The superiority of Liam Neeson, Ben Kingsley, and Ralph Fiennes stems from their ability to play each run-through of a take exactly the same. If the director does not introduce some changes, each run-through is a precise copy of the previous one. Our Polish actors are not always able to be that disciplined. Sometimes it is only a matter of seemingly invisible elements, such as the furrowing of a brow, but a director like Steven Spielberg will definitely notice. In the theater we value the fact that an actor does not make each performance a mechanical repetition of the one before. In film, however, such a creative approach to the role is not an asset. Doubtless, also, the language barrier hampers actors' performances when they must work in a language not native to them. Certainly, Andrzej Seweryn could comment on this subject, having recently reached a new height in his own career with a role he performed at the Comédie Française in Paris. But what strikes me most as I watch this international group of artists and technicians pool their talents and experience is that such an enterprise as ours can succeed because we are drawn by a compelling story and an inspired director.

8

Poldek

Jerry Molen expected that Poldek Page-Pfefferberg, because of his serious heart problems, would not arrive in Kraków on the set of *Schindler's List* before May, but I told Jerry, "You don't know Poldek. I bet he will be here in April, at the latest. After all, he just won't wait till you finish the film. I am sure the minute he feels better, he will not be able to sit still in one place." It was as I said. A week after his eightieth birthday, Poldek arrived in Kraków with his wife, Mila.

By then Spielberg had transferred his filming crew to Szeroka Street, which substitutes for Plac Zgody [Zgoda Square] in the original Kraków ghetto, liquidated fifty years ago. In March 1941, when all remaining Kraków Jews were ordered to move to the ghetto for "their safety," only twelve thousand of the original sixty-eight thousand there were left. By fall the number grew to seventeen thousand because some were brought from villages around Kraków, but on June 3, 1942, many thousands of Jews were deported from the ghetto to the death camp in Bełżec. Many hundreds were executed even before they were loaded onto the trains. Among those shot was a well-known Jewish poet, Mordechaj Gebirtig.

The next deportation, of seven thousand Jews, from Kraków to Bełżec took place in October 1942, and during that action six hundred Kraków Jews were murdered. The bloody liquidation of the Kraków ghetto took place on March 13 and 14, 1943. In those two days about two thousand people—the sick, the old, and the children—were slaughtered. About two thousand were transported to Birkenau, where 1,500 went immediately to gas chambers and 510 to the labor camp. About one thousand were force-marched to the camp in Płaszów. Tadeusz Pankiewicz, a Polish, non-Jewish pharmacist who ran Apteka Pod Orlem, the only pharmacy in the ghetto, left a dramatic description of what happened during the two days. He describes a heartbreaking scene when desperate mothers beg him for sleeping medications so that they can give it to their children and smuggle them to the Płaszów camp asleep in suitcases.

Szeroka Street, where Steven Spielberg decided to film the action which took place on the Plac Zgody fifty years ago, is actually a small square in the heart of the former Jewish section of Kraków called Kazimierz. There are three synagogues situated there. The oldest one in use is the Remuh Synagogue from the sixteenth century, and it is surrounded by the Remuh Cemetery. The Gothic synagogue, the so-called Old Synagogue, was dynamited by the Germans during the war. It was rebuilt in the fifties and now houses the Judaic department of the Kraków Museum of Town History. Also, the old ritual bath, or *mikveh*, was restored. On Szeroka Street archeologists and researchers into Kraków's past place the site of the first Jagiellonian University, founded by the Polish king Kazimierz the Great, in 1364. It is possible that old university cellars are still there under Szeroka Street.

A crowd of more than one thousand extras fills Szeroka Street. The street is surrounded by newly built ghetto walls in the characteristic shape of Jewish cemetery headstones, just as they were in the former ghetto in Podgórze. There is a short pause in filming scene 139, in which Tadeusz Pankiewicz, the pharmacist, is trying to carry a wounded Jewish woman to his pharmacy to administer first aid. A German soldier standing in front of the pharmacy shoots her in the head. Something went wrong with the special effects and the take has to be repeated. All the preparations have to start anew. A fresh explosive device must be attached to the actress's forehead; a tube from a container with artificial blood under her costume goes all the way to the kerchief on her head. Only when all that is ready can the command, "Action!" be given. The preparations take time, but the square, filled with a thousand people, is absolutely silent. They all hold their breaths. Finally, everything is ready. Spielberg orders: "ACTION!" Pankiewicz carries the unconscious but alive woman. The German orders him to put her down. Pankiewicz begs the soldier to let the woman into the pharmacy to dress her wounds. The German shoots the woman in the head and says to the pharmacist: "You, too, can join her." Blood spurts from the woman's head onto Pankiewicz. The woman's lifeless body hangs from his arms. I see the Pieta. There is silence on the street. Suddenly there is applause, and Ben Kingsley shouts, "Bravo!" I do not know if he wants to break the silence or to express his admiration for this dramatic scene.

I recall what he said to the students after the screening of *Gandhi* at the Wanda Theatre. He talked about the scene in which the suits were burnt. Thousands of extras took part in that scene. In the climactic moment about thirty thousand extras sitting on the ground rose as if in ecstasy. Two seasoned electricians observing the scene expressed their approval by uttering an expletive and adding, "It looks like we have a film!" They were not mistaken. Ben Kingsley added, "If it should happen on the set of a film I am making that at least one person voices an opinion as sincerely and precisely to the point as those two electricians did, then it's sure this film, too, will be successful." Is this exactly such a moment, and is Ben Kingsley's applause the spontaneous, sincere, and precise evaluation that signals good fortune for Steven Spielberg's film?

Poldek showed up on the set during a break before shooting a crowd scene on Szeroka Street. He had stopped at the hotel only long enough to leave his luggage in the rooms rented for him by the film company management. Mila preferred to remain there under the pretext that she had to unpack. Frankly, I was somewhat afraid of Poldek's first encounter with his past, so vividly reconstructed by Spielberg. Poldek is a person who could walk through walls just by sheer will power, as he proved many times, but I remember an incident when I almost made him cry.

It happened in 1985 in Kraków during the filming of our first documentary about Schindler and Poldek. We wandered through Kazimierz, through the area of the former labor camp in Płaszów and the former ghetto where Poldek lived from 1941 until 1943. We ended up in the Ghetto Museum on the Plac Zgody. It was here, at long last, that I asked Poldek what I thought was a simple question: "Why do you keep returning to Kraków, since you must associate these places with your and your loved ones' sufferings?" Poldek did not answer. I did not understand what happened, but I quickly realized that he was so emotionally stirred that he was not able to utter a word. He finally managed to take control of his emotions and in a breaking voice answered, "You see, America is a wonderful country, but to me it is like a stepmother, loving and wonderful, but still a stepmother, and Poland is and always will be a mother. Once in my life, as a young officer I pledged allegiance to her that I will always defend her, and I want to keep that promise." Silence. The television crew stood there in the museum, choked with emotion, unable to utter a sound.

I remembered that incident well, and so waited anxiously for the first encounter between Poldek and the film set. I was afraid for his heart, but everything turned out well. Spielberg had just arrived for a new take and he embraced Poldek the minute he saw him. So did other acquaintances from Los Angeles.

Ben Kingsley, whom the whole world recognizes, was in his

costume and makeup as Itzhak Stern. He stood almost at attention in front of Poldek and said, "Sir, permit me to introduce myself—Ben Kingsley." They stood together and talked for a long time.

Ralph Fiennes, in his uniform and a gray leather coat, joined them after a while, with hearty greetings. Later Poldek told me that seeing Ralph gave him goose pimples all over his body.

Jonathan Sagalle, who played Poldek, also came over. They sized each other up visually as if to form an opinion of each other's character. Although they are separated by a half a century in age and by a host of experiences, they seem to be similar psychologically. Soon thereafter I saw a prewar photo of Poldek in uniform; Jonathan was his spitting image.

That day Poldek stayed on the set for several hours, almost until the evening. We wandered through all kinds of niches and alleys, and he told me how his parents took him to the Old Synagogue. To this day he remembers the aroma of the apples they would smell to kill the feeling of hunger while fasting on the high holiday of Yom Kippur.

Among the extras on Szeroka Street, a small four-year-old, Genia, walks around in a red coat. She is a key image in the film script—a person who caused an inner change in Oskar Schindler. One could call her his conscience. In the first three hours of this black-and-white film, Genia will be the only color element on the screen in order to symbolically emphasize the meaning of that character in the change of the film's hero. Four-year-old Olivia Dąbrowska plays Genia. She is bored, tired, and maybe a little scared. At one point she rebels and cries, "I want my mama," but she quiets down in the arms of Steven, who treats her with the same paternal love as his own children, who sometimes visit the set.

Two hours later, though, when filming is finished, she really wants her mama. The next day there is a double ready—just in case.

The next day filming takes place on Lasota Hill. These are the scenes that had been scheduled to be filmed the previous Sunday but were canceled because of the sudden heavy snowfall. In the old days, the inhabitants of Kraków brought offerings here to honor their departed loved ones in a ceremony called Rękawka, but today it is the scene of the horseback ride Oskar Schindler and his mistress, Ingrid, took on March 13, 1943, the day they watched the liquidation of the Kraków ghetto. From there Oskar saw tiny Genia in a red coat, who walked unnoticed among the Hitler soldiers but as a witness to their crimes. That's when Schindler thought that if a child such as she perished he would be the only witness to the crime, and he decided to assume that role [of witness] and also to save as many Jews as he could for the future.

That's in the script. It is not certain that it really happened, but according to Mila Page, the girl in the red coat is an authentic figure. Steven Zaillian wrote it into the script and it was this version, the third, that most pleased Spielberg and was accepted by him.

This is one of the most dangerous takes. According to the book, the scene takes place just above Węgierska Street, but because the trees obscure the view from that point, the scene was moved further up toward the Austrian fort, close to the border of the former ghetto, where nothing would be in the way of the view. In the place where the scaffolds for the cameras were installed is a break in the wall of the old quarry. Below is a school yard on the bottom of the quarry and a fragment of the original ghetto wall, one of two still preserved. Liam Neeson, together with Beatrice Macola, who plays Ingrid, must ride their horses to the very edge of the precipice. The horses were rented from a riding stable. Liam is a good rider. Beatrice stays on a horse but she is not too sure of herself. During practice not long ago she fell off the horse, but anyone would feel insecure having to ride to the very edge of the hill. Everything has been done to insure safety for the actors in case the horses should spook. A few yards below is a flat piece of grass-covered shelflike land where safety netting has been installed. Several horse trainers stand by also. In other films, similar scenes would probably be performed by stunt people, but here, authenticity is pivotal to Spielberg's concept.

Marta, Schindler's girlfriend, whom I visited in New York, showed me photographs of Oskar riding on horseback, but not with Ingrid.

"This one sort of hunched up is Oskar and the other rider is Janina's husband," said Marta.

"Did you ride with Oskar?" I asked.

"Oh yes, but only one time and one time only. My horse bolted and I barely escaped alive, so I did not try again."

In Kraków, Janina showed me the same photograph. "My husband Zygmunt was an officer in the cavalry—no wonder he sat so straight on a horse," Janina said when I commented on the riding style of the two horsemen. "Actually, Schindler bought these horses so that my husband could ride with him."

"My husband," Janina reminisced, "was taken prisoner in Tomaszów Lubelski during the September campaign and was put in Oflag.* Soon afterward the Germans proclaimed that owners of agricultural land should be released so they could produce food for the Reich. My husband was supposed to be freed any day. We waited and waited but he did not show up. After a time we received a letter from somewhere in Germany, in which he described what happened. He had been released from Oflag and arrived in Kraków by a transport train. He got off, but some of his friends who were going to a different

---

*Oflag [a contraction of Offizierslager] refers to a special prison camp exclusively for military officers.

destination asked him to bring them some food. He obliged, making several trips to the train. Finally, on his eighth return, the German guards grabbed him, put him back on the transport train, and sent him again to Oflag for another year and a half. Then we got word that he was to have brain surgery. I was petrified. Schindler said to me, 'I will try to get him out.' He left, I don't know to where, but a week later my husband came home. He had to report to the Gestapo once a week and, though he was still involved with the Polish underground, he had a good alibi because he was employed by Schindler. Schindler evidently knew something, or maybe just suspected, because one day he turned to me and said, 'You know what, let him do whatever he thinks he must, but please don't let him use my car for that purpose,' and they did not stop their horseback rides together."

It is early on a misty Sunday morning in April. The filming of the scene on Lasota Hill is proceeding as scheduled. There is a slight rain from time to time, but it is not snowing like last week. The light drizzle does not interfere with filming, so everything can move according to plan. The filmed scene is silent; there is no dialogue between the actors. Whatever plays out below the hill in the Kraków ghetto speaks for itself. In the crowd of Kraków Jews dressed in dull gray worn-out garments one can clearly spot the red coat of little Genia. As usual, Spielberg strives to have several viewpoints on the same scene. First, it is Schindler and Ingrid approaching to the edge of the hill on horseback. Then a shot of both actors from the front and one from the back. Next, several shots of the streets in Podgórze, but with the two actors arranged in the frame so that the camera sees from behind their backs what is happening below. Finally, Spielberg orders a change to telephoto lenses, which are available in several lengths—300, 500, and 1000 millimeters—to film the scenes of the liquidation in close-ups from above.

Poldek and Mila arrive on the location during a break. They met fifty years ago in Kraków when Mila and her mother were ordered to leave Lódz, their hometown. Mila's mother, Dr. Maria Lewinson, was a well-known specialist in skin diseases and a founder of one of the first cosmetic institutes in Poland. The women chose to resettle in Kraków. Poldek fell in love with Mila at first sight, but he had to give his officer's word to a friend who had met Mila earlier that he would not pursue her. Later, the friend, seeing the great affection Poldek had for Mila, released him from the vow during a New Year's Eve party. Now they had to convince Mila's mother, who opposed their plans because she did not think that those times were suitable for getting engaged. Poldek, however, never was one to give up easily. He tried to persuade his future mother-in-law for several hours, and finally, around three in the morning, she gave up. Poldek and Mila had many dates here on Krzemionki fifty years ago.

Now, on the same Krzemionki, they meet their film counterparts. Anna Maria Stein arranged the meeting so that the film crew from Universal making a documentary (also in black-and-white) about the filming of Spielberg's *Schindler's List* could record the event. Poldek had already met Jonathan Sagalle the day before, when he visited the set. Mila is portrayed by a young Israeli actress, Adi Nitzan, whom Mila took a liking to from first sight.

"You are so beautiful," she cried out when she first saw Adi, and the real Poldek added, proud as a peacock, "My Mila also was beautiful. That's why I married her, though all the girls I taught in high school were in love with me."

Steven Spielberg walks up to Poldek and Mila. In Los Angeles they had spent many hours talking about Oskar and their life in Kraków during the war. Mila conveys greetings to Steven from his mother. They go to the same hairdresser in Los Angeles. Steven introduces his wife. Liam Neeson joins the group, and the Pages meet him for the first time. They agree that he is an excellent choice. Liam's physique reminds them of Oskar

Schindler. In a moment, Poldek leads Steven to the edge of the hill to show him "his" Podgórze. "I am a boy from Podgórze," he explains. "I was born on Lwowska Street in a house next to the Baroque statue of Our Father, still standing there, and in that school, there below us, I learned how to read and write. Later, I went to the Podgórze high school named after Tadeusz Kościuszko. We were very proud to wear our school caps with white and red bands," Poldek concludes.

A while later I am invited to join Poldek, Mila, Spielberg, Liam, Jonathan, and Adi for a "family" photograph. I return with Poldek and Mila to the hotel because it is freezing cold, muddy, and wet on the Lasota Hill. Our boots are soaked. Spielberg and his crew move down into the streets of Podgórze in order to film from a different position what Oskar observed from atop the hill.

On Thursday, Andrzej Wajda and his wife, scene designer Krystyna Zachwatowicz*, arrive on Spielberg's set in the television studio in Łęg. A year ago when they met, Andrzej Wajda told Spielberg that his dream had been to once in his lifetime make a film in the American style of super-production. To that Spielberg answered that he always wanted to make a modest, black-and-white film in the European style. Steven is now in the process of realizing his dream. At Universal they tried to talk him out of making a black and white film, though. Universal argued that black-and-white films do not sell well on videocassettes, which on their own bring in profits comparable to movie theater ticket sales. Also, television networks are reluctant to buy black-and-white films. Spielberg stubbornly defended his idea and finally won.

---

*Krystyna Zachwatowicz is among Poland's most respected scene designers. She has created many noted designs, including several for stage productions directed by her husband.

When Andrzej Wajda and his wife arrive in the studio, accompanied by Lew Rywin, the filming of a segment involving the reconstructed interior of Amon Goeth's villa is in progress. One has to wait a few minutes for a break. A director's chair with Wajda's name on it is brought in. Spielberg had anticipated the visit and ordered such a personalized chair. For Krystyna Zachwatowicz a chair with the sign "actor" was found. The two great film makers greet each other affectionately. The next scene is ready to shoot, and Spielberg invites everybody to accompany him onto the set.

After a while they are joined by Poldek, who has had to spend a few days in bed. He came down with the flu after visiting the filming on Krzemionki in the rain last Sunday. Poldek greets Wajda with great respect. He tells him that before Universal bought the rights to filming *Schindler's List*, he was dreaming that Wajda might be engaged to do it. He even began certain negotiations with Metro-Goldwyn-Mayer. Now, he is very happy that he can at last meet Wajda—on Spielberg's movie set.

We are watching the action on the set. Oskar Schindler plays a game of blackjack with Amon Goeth. The stakes are 14,000 marks and a Jewish woman, Helena Hirsch, who was chosen by Amon to work in his villa. The part of Helena is portrayed by an Israeli actress, Embeth Davidtz. Amon Goeth is dealing. First the camera registers Schindler's reactions, then it focuses on Goeth. Finally, a close-up on the cards from above: 9 of clubs, 7 of diamonds—that shows 16. Amon, smiling, offers another. Oskar hesitates—stay or draw? Daring convention and all odds, he takes it (ordinarily, a sucker move)—an Ace of Hearts! Amon has no choice, he's dealing and *must* draw, but with two cards already, what are his odds on beating 17?—he draws a Jack and loses. The name of Helena Hirsch is now added to Schindler's list. Today the real Helena lives in Israel. Spielberg repeats the scene several times; he changes camera positions, changes lenses. This way he has wider possibilities for editing. On the set we see one seemingly long scene, on the screen we

will see a dynamic montage building suspense to the climax—
Amon Goeth's losing scream.

The next scene will be realized in a different room of the
Amon Goeth villa, also reconstructed in the Łęg studio. Liam
Neeson and Ralph Fiennes take a short break to concentrate.

We move to the parlor of the reconstructed villa. Poldek is
sitting there with an album of old photos from the war, which
he brought with him. Among the photos are snaps of Amon
Goeth, but not in uniform, just a private person sleeping on a
lawn chaise on the terrace of his villa in Płaszów. Another photo
shows Amon's famous vicious dogs. Ralph Fiennes is interested
in everything pertaining to the character he portrays. He looks
at Poldek's album, page after page, and listens to the tales about
the photos. It is evident that they were made by someone very
close to Amon Goeth, someone who had an access to him at all
times, even when Amon was in an undershirt and house
slippers. There are also pictures of the Płaszów camp prisoners
and of the camp itself.

Poldek begins to tell a story about the album:

While working as a welder in Amon Goeth's garage, I
noticed a German by the name of Rajmund Titsch taking
photographs. Titsch was helping Madritsch, the owner of a
factory in the Płaszów concentration camp that produced
uniforms for the Wehrmacht. I noticed that Titsch was
taking the pictures all over the camp—but secretly, as if he
were hiding the fact. I lost contact with Titsch when I left
Płaszów for Brinnlitz with Oskar Schindler. Well, in 1963, I
find out that he lives in Vienna. I go there, seek him out,
and I tell him, "Mr. Titsch, I know that you were taking
photographs in the Płaszów camp. I have to have the
photographs." At first, he completely denies everything. I
get the impression that he is afraid of something. For a
long time I try to convince him. Finally, I take out five
hundred dollars and promise him any kind of help he
might need, such as getting medication which could not be

obtained in Europe. That must have convinced him; his wife was ill and needed medicines which were available only in the States. He warned me, however, that I was entering into very risky business. He had never developed the negatives. Right after the war he buried them, and who knows what's left of them after almost twenty years. "I agree," I say, "I'm doing it at my own risk." Then he gives me another condition: I could not publish the pictures until after his death. He was afraid of repercussions from ODESSA, the organization that helped former SS men have a new start after the war. I promise. We go to a small square where Titsch had buried the negatives in a metal box next to some statue. In it are three rolls of Agfa film.

I took the next flight to Jerusalem, where the following day we developed the precious film in the Yad Vashem Museum laboratory. All the pictures were excellent in spite of being in the ground for twenty years. We obtained one hundred six unique photographs.

First, only Liam Neeson and Ralph Fiennes sit next to Poldek while he is telling his story, but soon there are many more listeners. Steven Spielberg joins them and looks at the album over Poldek's shoulder, though he has seen the pictures before. Andrzej Wajda also is fascinated by the account, especially since Poldek is a wonderful story teller. Steven Tate, the assistant cameraman with whom I spent a Sunday some time ago tracing Schindler's activities in Kraków, has to stand on a chair in order to see the contents of the album, and the crowd around Poldek is growing. David James is taking pictures of the group: Who knows if such a gathering of film heroes and creators ever will take place again? The scene I observe is like a vein of pure gold—very seldom is one found.

I glance at Steven and the producers for signs of annoyance that Poldek caused such a long break in the filming. One of the assistants gives Spielberg a sign that everybody will be ready to start filming in five minutes. Steven nods his head, acknowledging. So it is obvious that spontaneity on the set of an American film is strictly controlled. No wonder, since each hour the crew is on the set costs $6,000. Soon I hear a command: "Crew number one on the set! Action!"

On Saturday I went with Poldek and Mila to the set at Oskar Schindler's former factory on Lipowa Street in the Zabłocie area. There we found George Lucas, who came to Kraków for only a half day just to spend a bit of time on Steven Spielberg's location. For many years, Spielberg and Lucas have been friends, collaborators, and, in a sense, rivals. Lucas's *Star Wars* (1977) earned $180 million dollars, in second place after *E.T.*, but *The Young Indiana Jones Chronicles* (1992) thirty-episode series was produced for television by Lucas at Spielberg's Amblin Entertainment. During the Oscar ceremonies in 1982, it was Steven Spielberg who handed the American Film Directors Guild award to George Lucas for creative accomplishments.

When Poldek arrived on the set he immediately noticed that the set dressers forgot to place a letter *F* above the entrance with the other two letters standing for D.E.F., the short form of the name for Schindler's factory. A photograph by Rajmund Titsch from 1943 shows Oskar Schindler surrounded by beautiful women and other workers. They were celebrating the fourth anniversary of the opening of Emalia, the popular name for Schindler's factory. The columns on each side of the gate were decorated with fir branches. There were also German flags with swastikas. Spielberg decided to reconstruct that moment in his film, but it would mean a need for some action just before and after the taking of the photo. Soon it became clear why the letter *F* was missing.

The scene, as conceived by Spielberg, begins with the mounting of the missing letter above the gate. Oskar Schindler, surrounded by his beautiful secretaries, led by Victoria Klonowska, is watching the workers completing the task. When the last nail is pounded in, everybody applauds and turns around to pose for the souvenir picture. The photographer approaches the women to place them in a pleasing composition. At the same time, Schindler walks up to the camera, looks at the image on the ground-glass, shows his displeasure with the setup, and then moves the camera two meters to one side. As the photographer returns, he becomes angry. After all, in this case, he is the artist and wants to move the camera back where he originally placed it. Schindler motions to him that the camera should stay where Schindler placed it. Steven dreamed up that little scenario literally at the last minute. He explains to the extra who portrays the photographer: "Behave like an artist and not like a handyman; don't let anybody start changing your creation!" It was just as if I was hearing Steven Spielberg's credo.

The next scene required a change in location. The camera was placed in the yard of the factory to record the arrival of Schindler: The gate opened and Schindler arrived in his car—a black Horche. Across the street, a tall wooden fence screened a modern building built in the eighties. There was a small amount of artificial snow. This was the only take in *Schindler's List* where artificial snow had to be used. In all the other scenes, one could depend on Mother Nature. During the preparations, Spielberg sat down in his director's chair for a moment of quiet next to George Lucas. I do not know what the two geniuses of modern film talked about on Zabłocie Street in Kraków's Podgórze. They sat there and no one bothered them. A year ago if some one were to have told me that I would see a Martian coming out of a flying saucer on Lipowa Street, I would think, Who knows, anything is possible, but if I had been told that I would meet Steven Spielberg and George Lucas here together, I certainly would have said, "That's impossible!"

Monday is the last day in Kraków for Poldek and Mila. The next day they leave for Paris and then Los Angeles. After a morning of shooting the scenes on Szeroka Street, the film crew move for a few days to the enamelware factory in Olkusz that will be the location for the interior scenes of the Kraków Emalia. The Pages wish to say goodbye to Steven, so we are going to Olkusz, about forty-nine miles from Kraków. Michael Gordon, a German actor from Munich, is accompanying us. He plays the part of Mr. Nussbaum, a Kraków Jew who, according to the Schindler legend, was paid by Oskar for his apartment on Straszewskiego Street. Supposedly for that money, Nussbaum bought his family an exit from occupied Poland to somewhere in southern Europe. Michael Gordon, whose ancestors were Wilno Jews, is a well-known actor in theater and film. In Kraków he developed a habit of spending his evenings at the theater, so he became friends with many of Kraków's actors. His film partner is Aldona Grochal, portraying Mrs. Nussbaum.

On the way to Olkusz we stop in the picturesque village of Pieskowa Skała for *bigos*, a typically Polish stew with cabbage, meat, sausage, bacon, mushrooms, and tomatoes. During the meal, Michael confesses that he has another skill which he practices with passion—cooking. No wonder that as we sit eating and listening to recipes for the best *bigos*, time passes pleasantly but too quickly.

When we arrive in Olkusz, Steven Spielberg has just finished filming the first scene at that location. The set is in an unused factory space which contains everything necessary for the sequence. There are hydraulic presses to stamp out pots from round discs of sheet metal; there are also two ovens for baking enamel. Only a few old tables, some anvils, and polishing wheels needed to be added. The Olkusz factory workers taught the women extras to polish metal so that streams of bright sparks were flying. Old huge pressure gauges were installed on gas pipes. On the second floor there was a small three-room office with windows overlooking the factory hall, which permitted Schindler to observe the factory activities during production. During filming in the interior of the office, the camera could also record what Schindler saw below where the workers pushed carts with stamped but not yet enameled vessels, while others performed various tasks at worktables. There was also a large table used for meals.

During a break for scene changes, Mila and Poldek say goodbye to Steven. They have brought him a present: a beautiful painting by Paweł Vogler, a son of their Kraków friends. The title is *The Wall*, and it was inspired by the fate of the Jews a half century ago. Against the background of a wall, in blacks, browns, and reds, there is a white Torah.*

"Too bad the whole painting is not black-and-white," says Spielberg. That's an indirect reference to *Schindler's List* being filmed in black-and-white. "The Holocaust," he says, "was life without light. For me the symbol of life is color. That's why a film about the Holocaust has to be in black-and-white."

While saying goodbye to the Pages, Spielberg says, "See you in Jerusalem next month." This is a takeoff on an old Jewish greeting which goes, "Next year in Jerusalem." By saying that, a wish is expressed that all the Jews from the Diaspora† will meet in their own country. Now, Spielberg's wish has additional significance. It points to his plan of gathering in Jerusalem all the authentic heroes of his film, the real Schindler Jews, and filming them together with the actors who recreated their characters. This will occur at Oskar Schindler's tomb, on which each of them is to place a stone, as is customary in Jewish tradition.

---

*The Torah is the Jewish scripture—the five books of Moses, also called the Pentateuch. These books of scripture are written on a large sacred scroll kept within the Ark of the Altar in the Temple.

†Diaspora refers to the body of Jews scattered throughout the world, wandering without a Palestinian homeland, after their Babylonian captivity.

9

Niusia

We are going to Olkusz with Niusia Karakulska, born Niusia Horowitz. Today Steven Spielberg is there filming the scene of Oskar Schindler's birthday celebration and Niusia will be the heroine. During their first meeting, Spielberg asked Niusia to come to the set today.

The Horowitz family lived on Wawrzyńca Street in the part of Kraków called Kazimierz. Like many other Polish citizens, the whole family left for the East at the start of the war. They went as far as Janów near Lublin. However, after September 17 the Horowitz family returned and made their home in Bochnia [a town closer to Kraków], where Niusia's uncle lived. They stayed there until the opening of the Kraków ghetto in March 1941. Then they joined the twelve thousand Kraków Jews who were to live in the ghetto. Miraculously, when the ghetto was liquidated two years later, they were among the one thousand Jews transferred to the camp in Płaszów. Niusia was only eleven, but her birth certificate was altered to thirteen so the young girl would be qualified to work. Her parents worked for Schindler. When Oskar Schindler moved "his" Jews to Brinnlitz, Niusia and her mother Regina were among the Schindler women taken by mistake to Birkenau; her father Dolek and younger brother Ryszard ended up in Auschwitz. Niusia, her mother, and the rest of those three hundred women arrived in Brinnlitz in the beginning of November 1944. Oskar Schindler had been expecting them and was there to greet them.

On his birthday, April 28, 1945, a few days before the end of the war in Europe, the Schindler Jews baked a cake out of rye flour and presented it to their savior with best wishes. Niusia was the one who wished him "Happy Birthday" in the name of all present. To this day she remembers the text of her speech.*

It is a coincidence that the day we ride to the location for filming Oskar Schindler's birthday is also Niusia's birthday. The first one to congratulate her is Ben Kingsley, who kisses her on both cheeks. Then Steven Spielberg does the same and adds, "I already finished filming your scene."

That scene was conceived during the first meeting between Niusia and Spielberg, on the first real spring Sunday in March 1993. The sun is warm and the temperature was above 68°F. We are dressed warmly, expecting no change in the weather, so now it is a pleasure to peel off layers of warm clothing. Spielberg has been shooting a scene on the Kraków Rynek Główny [the main square]. Oskar Schindler is to drive onto the square in his newly purchased car. Then, as on such occasions many years ago, he will be surrounded by his lovely secretaries, including Victoria Klonowska, and champagne will flow like water.

When we enter the Rynek, Niusia grabs my hand and freezes in place. She must have been shocked by the view: German soldiers are milling around the Rynek, canvas topped military trucks are parked in a column; and right next to us are motorcycles with machine guns mounted on them. For me it is simply a set for the film, but for Niusia these are real and painful memories. Fortunately, Spielberg has just finished

---

*The text of Niusia's speech is found at the beginning of chapter 37 in Thomas Keneally's *Schindler's List*.

filming and the whole crew and equipment already have moved
to another location. Among the stands of flower vendors we
meet Miki Stanisiç. I ask if he knows where one may find
Spielberg. "Yes, I know exactly within ten yards," says Miki.
After all, it is my 'job' to keep track of him. Go to Mikołajska
Street, turn left on Krzyża Street, and Spielberg is standing
there within ten yards of the intersection."

In a few minutes we find the Master exactly as directed. He is
getting ready to shoot a scene based on old photos saved from
the war. These old photographs show a group of exhilarated
German soldiers surrounding a few Orthodox Jews and cutting
off their *peyes* [curled side locks worn by Orthodox Jewish men].
Spielberg is filming this scene with a moving camera. In
Schindler's List he often brings to life such scenes, known from
documentary photos, which grew and became embedded in our
memories as archetypes. There is a pause in the shooting. I
approach Steven with Niusia and introduce her. "Steven, this is
Niusia Karakulska; Niusia Horowitz in your film. She is the girl
who wished Oskar Schindler 'Happy Birthday.'" I really did not
have to finish the sentence because no one knows the script
better than Steven. Steven greets his guest warmly. Niusia
understands English but does not speak it well, so I am the
interpreter. Steven takes the opportunity to ask Niusia about
details that are important but not found in Thomas Keneally's
book. What were they wearing? What did they eat in Schindler's
factory? What kind of bread were they given? What kind of
marmalade? Details, details, details—Spielberg loves details.
Niusia opens Keneally's book; in the author's note, he thanks
the people whose recollections helped him write the book. She
points to the names mentioned by Keneally and says: "Regina
Horowitz is my mother, Henry Rosner is my uncle, Mancy
[Mariana] Rosner is my aunt, Ryszard Horowitz my brother,
Olek Rosner my cousin, Leo Rosner my other uncle, and
Niusia—that's me."

"This is unbelievable," Steven ponders. "This looks like a
miracle. Until now I was always hearing from various Jews, 'My

mother perished; my father perished; my whole family; all my
relatives were murdered,' and here I am hearing something
unbelievable: the whole family survived."

"This does not just look like a miracle," Niusia corrects him.
"This is a miracle. A miracle caused by Oskar Schindler."

"Did he take money or jewelry from you?" Spielberg asks.

"Not at all," Niusia answers, "but one time I survived thanks
to a diamond my mother had."

"How did that happen?" Spielberg asks.

"It was when we were in Auschwitz-Birkenau. Three times I
was on the way to the gas chamber," Niusia explains. "One time
mother hid me in the chimney of a stove that was not in use;
another time she bribed an SS woman with a diamond which
she had been able to swallow earlier when they were deporting
us. I don't know what happened the third time, because my
mother did not tell anything in detail—but she said that I had
been marked for the gas chamber, again."

I have known Niusia for many years and I thought that I
knew her life history by heart, but she never mentioned the
stories she just told Steven. I cannot be jealous; evidently Steven
awoke a special trust so that she decided to tell him her most
intimate biographical details from having been on the brink of
life and death.

"Tell me more about the story of the diamond," Spielberg
says. "Did such things happen often in the ghetto?"

"I think so," Niusia answers.

"If you'll permit me, I'll add this scene to the script. When
you see it in the film," Spielberg adds, "remember this will be
your scene." So scene 126a was conceived, introduced into the
ninth set of changes to the script, and written on gray pages:

126a   INTERIOR: AN APARTMENT
IN THE GHETTO—DAWN   126a

A man quickly tears off a piece of wallpaper, exposing a
small opening in the wall. The small hand of a boy pulls

out a tiny bundle tied up with a string. At the table, with the family around, the man opens the bundle, exposing its contents: a few rings, necklaces, a small broach, un-mounted precious stones. He takes a piece of bread, wraps it around the little broach, puts it in his mouth, and swallows while drinking water.

Loud German voices echo in the building. Each member of the family grabs a piece of jewelry, wraps it in bread, and swallows. The wife looks at her wedding ring, takes it off her finger, and swallows quickly with the bread. The boy looks at this unusual family meal and this moment stays in his memory forever.

This is how the scene that Niusia Karakulska helped create was conceived. I remember another unusual moment from our meeting that day. They were filming another scene: Poldek (Jonathan Sagalle) is walking on Mikołajska Street. He walks up to a bookstore window (in it is displayed Adolf Hitler's *Mein Kampf*, which I loaned for the film). Inconspicuously, he takes off the white armband with the blue Star of David in order to be able to go to the city on some business for Schindler. At the same moment the clock bell in the steeple of Marjacki Bazylika [St. Mary's Basilica] strikes 12:00 noon, then the bells ring in the small church of Panna Maria on Gródek, calling the faithful for a noontime prayer. A moment later the trumpeter plays the Hejnal from the Marjacki steeple. This scene in the film has no dialogue. If one had wanted to incorporate all of these sound effects into the script it would seem to require a real effort for perfect timing. Here, everything rang without anyone coordinating. It was the magic of Kraków—exactly at noon.*

---

*Every hour immediately after the hour bell, a trumpeter plays a tune called the Hejnal from the steeple of Majacki Bazylika. "Hejnal" is a plain melody built around five notes and was used in medieval times as a warning alarm. The trumpet is played four times, once each from windows on the points of the compass. This occurs twenty-four hours a day. The custom appears to have begun in medieval times

A month after their first meeting in Kraków, Niusia is back on the set—this time at the factory in Olkusz. Steven explains that he often creates one person for the film out of several actual historical persons. He makes similar use of situations. For example, he can combine several independent occurrences into one. This will happen with the scene of Oskar Schindler's birthday celebration. Steven decided to combine two occurrences in the life of Schindler into one to increase the dramatic impact. The first concerns an incident when Schindler first opened his factory in Kraków. In a mood to celebrate, he let himself passionately kiss a beautiful Jewish female worker in his factory. He was denounced to the Gestapo for having broken the law of racial purity and spent a couple of days in the Gestapo prison on Pomorska Street. The second occurrence was his birthday party, when Niusia congratulated him. Schindler kissed her also—on both cheeks. Today, in the filmed scene, two actresses will take part: Niusia, portrayed by Agnieszka Makuszewska and a grown-up young, unnamed Jewish woman portrayed by beautiful Magdalena Dondurian, who is part Armenian—and looking so lovely that I would not be surprised if Schindler wanted to kiss her. Spielberg explains to Niusia why he decided on such a scheme. He needs a passionate kiss to enhance the dramatic action, but an actor should not kiss an underage girl on the mouth because the audience may perceive it as an act of molesting, which has complicated the reception of

---

after a time when, according to legend, a watchman on the tower saw signs of an approaching Tartar army bent on conquering the city, took up a trumpet, and began playing the Hejnal. By doing so, he managed to arouse enough of the city to muster a force which eventually drove off the Tartars and saved Kraków. Legend says the trumpeter was stopped in mid-phrase by a Tartar arrow. So, when the trumpeter plays, he stops mid-phrase after beginning the second repeat of the melody. Everyone who visits Kraków today goes at least once to Rynek Główny, the old central square of the medieval city, on the corner of which is Marjacki Bazylika, to hear the trumpeter—part of the "magic of Kraków."

more than one American film. Spielberg did not want to add years to Niusia and thus invent a new person, so he preferred to add another, older girl.

Everything is ready to begin shooting. In Oskar Schindler's office overlooking the factory floor the tables are loaded with party food: hams, sausages, chocolates, pineapples, bottles of Rhine wine, and cognac. Schindler is hosting guests representing the German administration, who in turn are being entertained by his beautiful secretaries. Itzhak Stern is present. Amon Goeth has brought his "court" musicians—the brothers Rosner; they are playing a Jewish melody. A beautiful torte with marzipan roses is added to the table—a gift from the office workers. Victoria Klonowska asks Oskar to make a wish. He answers that all his wishes already have come true. Toast. Schindler kisses all women present. All of a sudden there is silence. Two girls from Schindler's Jews enter, their drab dresses in contrast to the exquisite garments of the other guests. The girls bring in a small dark cake slightly squashed, which is the present from the workers in the Emalia factory. The cake is not pretty. Just before filming this scene Spielberg had the torte squashed because, for his taste, it looked too nice. Caesar Diez Alva, a long-haired Basque, is one of the two prop masters and thus always present. He went to work immediately and fixed the cake so that it did not look as if it had come straight from a bakery.

The whole scene with the cake actually took place in Brinnlitz and not in Kraków, but then the dramatic sequence of kissing a Jewish girl and all the complications that followed could not have taken place in Brinnlitz. The real present-day Niusia is standing in a narrow passage between the two halls and is watching the first take. I am standing next to her, but I am really absorbed in the proceedings. When the first take is finished I look around for Niusia—she has disappeared. I find her sitting in a corner of the small office trying to hide her distress. Steven, too, is looking for her. He approaches me, and pointing at Niusia he asks, "What happened?" Then he walks up to Niusia, embraces her and holds her in his arms for a long time. Liam Neeson follows him and kisses the shaken Niusia on both cheeks—just as Oskar Schindler did years ago.

The Schindler birthday scene is repeated many times. It is filmed from all possible angles. Liam Neeson, included in *People* magazine's annual supplement, "The Fifty Most Beautiful People in the World" [May 3, 1993], is kissing and is kissed, endlessly. After each take, the makeup artist has to correct his makeup and wipe off the traces of lipstick left by the kissing secretaries. When it seems that everything the director wants is done, Steven suddenly says, "I have a new idea for this scene," and it starts from the beginning. The scene opens as before with the beautifully decorated cake being brought in, followed by the little actress portraying Niusia and her grown-up friend carrying in the small dark cake. When Schindler is kissing the Jewish woman, which causes dismay among the guests, the silence is broken by the Rosner brothers, who start to play a popular song, "This Last Sunday." This was supposed to be only an instrumental played on an accordion and violin, but Jacek Wójcicki spontaneously joins in with his vocal renditions, to the applause of the actors and all others present. [Spielberg must have liked the result of this spontaneity, because in the film it is a take, with Jacek Wójcicki singing to end the scene.]

We are sitting in a small office upstairs. Through the glass windows looking out on the factory hall we can see the Schindler Jews preparing for an evening meal. In a corner there is a Christmas tree. Niusia remembers that in Brinnlitz, instead of colorful balls and angel hair, which of course were not available, it was decorated with metal shavings which were left after the manufacturing of some metal vessels.

Not long ago Spielberg told an American reporter on CBS Television that for many years around Christmastime he had a complex resulting from his Jewish heritage. In the small town where he lived as a child, his was the only Jewish family in a Christian neighborhood. When Christmas approached, all the neighbors' houses were decorated with blinking lights. His house was sad, with a dark porch lit by a single small lamp. Steven often asked his father if maybe he could change the plain porch light bulb into a colorful one—maybe a red one. For a long time, he remembered it this way. It was only a few years ago that he became interested in his roots—now with great pride.

We look at the factory hall below. There is a conveyor with hooks on which freshly turned milk cans are hanging. They are not enameled as yet. Niusia takes a small metal box made of thin sheet metal out of her purse. This is her only souvenir from Brinnlitz. Somebody made it for her as a gift—she does not remember who. It is her trinket box—a relic from the past.

Steven Spielberg, together with a special-effects expert, approaches Niusia again. He wants to know if she remembers the crematorium chimneys in Birkenau. Did they spew just smoke or were flames also seen? In the evening they will be filming smoke over Birkenau and Spielberg wants to know exactly how it looked. Niusia remembers black smoke through which sometimes one could see bluish yellow flames and sparks. The special-effects expert nods. He already knows which chemicals to add to the fire to get the result desired by the director.

Branko Lustig sits down next to us. He, too, remembers bluish yellow flames. He is the same age as Niusia and a fellow prisoner from Auschwitz. When Niusia first came to the set on Krzyża Street, Branko offered her a single red rose. Branko wonders if Niusia sometimes feels that all the horrors that happened to her in the past were just a nightmare in a deep sleep. Niusia denies it. For her the past is still as real and alive as if it happened yesterday.

"For me," says Branko, "especially when I go skiing in the mountains or swimming in the ocean, the past feels like a distant nightmare, but when I look at the tattoo on my arm, everything comes back and I know it is a horrible truth."

A few months ago, when the Foundation for Polish-German Reconciliation began reviewing the applications by former concentration camp inmates requesting reparations, Niusia also submitted an application. The computer rejected her name, however. Niusia had submitted her real date of birth, which was two years less than the one she falsified during the war. It is thanks to this lie that she survived. As an eleven-year-old girl she had no chance, but as a thirteen-year-old she could—and was forced to—work. The computer said the person named Niusia Karakulska, born Horowitz, who celebrated her sixty-first birthday on the day Spielberg filmed "her" scene, simply did not exist. So, Steven Spielberg wrote in Niusia's copy of the book *Schindler's List*: "How good it is that you are alive!"

10

I Act, Therefore I Am

One day Magdalena Szwarcbart, the casting director for *Schindler's List,* asked me if I would play a German official in the film. My answer was that in Spielberg's film I'll even play a wall. Quite a bit of time passed after that conversation, so I came to the conclusion that it was all over, especially since I found out that Lew Rywin was asked in an interview by Jurek Armata if he, too, would like to take a part in an episode, as was Branko Lustig. Lew said that it was a possibility and submitted to a screen test. Nobody invited me to have a screen test—too bad, I thought, they probably found someone else.

In the meantime there was an opportunity to play a colonel, or maybe even a German general, as a member of a 1944 military court before whom Schindler testified in a corruption case. The accused was Amon Goeth. The scene was filmed in the office of the president of Kraków on a Saturday. When Branko arrived on the set to check out the extras who were to play the members of the court, he became furious. Out of seven, only three were of an age appropriate to wear a uniform with the insignia of a colonel or general. The rest were young men who, at best, could pass for second lieutenant. "Please find some men of the right age immediately," he ordered. The assistants to the director scattered all over, running to cafes in search of older extras. One of the assistants asked me in passing if I would like to perform. "Of course," I said, but evidently he did not hear a word of it as he rushed by, intent on checking out the customers in Cafe Noworola. It seemed that my last opportunity to be an actor in a Spielberg film had just disappeared up the street.

Then Monday, April 26, Magdalena asked me if I could play a clerk the next day. "You have spoken," I said. I was supposed to arrive in the studio in Łęg at 7:00 A.M. the next day to be fitted for a costume. I was so nervous I could not sleep all night, but I rationalized that it was the hot weather. Well, I asked for it. In the morning there was a mob of extras waiting in front of the costume shop who had been told to come at 5:00 A.M. I did not have to wait my turn in line. Such are the privileges of a "star" in an episode; I had a few lines to speak. The wardrobe worker asked who my character was, and I told her, "A clerk, not in a uniform." She looked me over, skillfully estimated my measurements, and handed me a Tyrolean-style jacket. I put it on. It fit perfectly, but she was not satisfied. "It is too 'German,'" she decided. "Let's try something else." She took a double-breasted gray suit off a hanger. I like double-breasted suits. It was a little tight in the waist, but what would one not do for art? I needed a hat to complete the outfit. The first two were too small; the third was a bit too large, but it would do. "Perfect," I said, when she asked how it felt.

The costume designer for *Schindler's List* was Anna Biedrzycka-Sheppard, born in Warsaw, and who had been living for many years in London. She designed costumes for Krzysztof Zanussi and Janusz Morgenstern, among others, and for Agnieszka Holland's film *To Kill a Priest* (1988).

I ride to the location with Steven and Brian, two Americans who are my partners in the scene. They differ from me because they are clerks in German uniforms. I am glad I do not wear a uniform. Brian and Steven are American volunteers, economists educated in American universities, who came to Poland for a year to help Polish enterprises struggling with problems caused by the transformation of the economy. I joke with them that instead of teaching the Polish businessmen how to make money they are making money playing in Spielberg's film.

Magdalena Szwarcbart is waiting for us on the set on Kamienna Street and directs us to the makeup studio. This is located in a specially-equipped bus and has four comfortable armchairs. One wall of the bus is covered by a mirror surrounded by numerous photographs of cast members in their makeup, big stars, and amateurs like myself. In my case I need to have my hair trimmed only a bit, I'd been to a barber two weeks before. Ben Kingsley comes in. Because he has to wear a wig, putting on his makeup takes a little longer. The makeup designer for *Schindler's List* is Christina Smith. She received an Oscar nomination for Spielberg's *Hook* (1991). She also designed makeup for *Hero* (1992), *Steel Magnolias* (1989), *Blaze* (1989), *Black Rain* (1989), and *New York, New York* (1977).

Leaving the makeup bus, I go by the "Club," also located in a specially-outfitted bus. This is a lounge for actors in the episodes. There are comfortable armchairs, TV sets, VCRs, a bar with excellent espresso coffee, and a mini-bathroom. This, like the other production busses, was borrowed from an outfit in Zagreb, Yugoslavia. Branko Lustig waves at me from the Club. Branko was with Zagreb Film for thirty years as an American coproducer in the making of many prominent films. Zagreb specialized in coproducing films. Now, because of the civil war in the former Yugoslavia, nobody wants to make films there. The professional crews are unemployed and expensive special equipment sits unused. In turn, Polish private firms specializing in serving film productions are in their infancy, only just being started. It is no wonder that Spielberg's company utilizes known, experienced companies. There is no time for experimentation: Each shooting day costs $60,000, and if *Schindler's List* can be produced efficiently, other directors will follow Spielberg's steps. Then, maybe in a year or two, instead of motor busses from Zagreb there will be others from Warsaw's Heritage Films. In the meantime, only a very quiet electric generator needed for huge spotlights is supplied by the Warsaw firm. There are also specialized vehicles from the Karkowski Eurotrans Car Company in Chylice, near Warsaw. Karkowski Eurotrans is the first privately owned company in Poland specializing in providing special transport in support of filmmaking.

I walk back to Branko Lustig, who is laughing, looking at my double-breasted suit and the fedora on my head. "Well," he says, "it's now my turn to laugh." This is his small revenge and an allusion to my having made funny faces when Branko also played a small part—the maître d'hôtel in a Kraków restaurant. I sit in the lounge with Brian and Steven waiting for our call. We're not supposed to leave unless we notify Zdravko Madsarevic, who is responsible for the presence of the actors whenever they are required on the set. In walks Ossi Ragheb, who oversees the dialogue in the film. He is supposed to rehearse our pronunciation of the lines. The fragment from the shooting script I was given for my part in scene 95 is as follows:

95   EXTERIOR: PROKOCIM DEPOT— KRAKÓW—NIGHT   95

From the locomotive, looking back, the string of slatted livestock carriages stretches into darkness. There's a lot of activity on the platform: Guards mill. Handcarts piled with luggage trundle by. People hand up children to others already in the cars and climb aboard after them. Soldiers and clerks are supervising the boarding of hundreds of Jews onto the train.

CLERKS

> Your luggage will follow you. Make sure
> it's clearly labeled. Leave your luggage on
> the platform.

I will stand on the platform with my two American partners

and we are to recite the three sentences. Oskar Schindler arrives at the train station. He has found out that his "right hand," Itzhak Stern, was caught in the ghetto and sent to the station. Schindler is trying to find him and pull him out of the transport.

Ossi is supposed to coach Brian and Steven in losing their American accents. They are to speak English with a German or at least some European accent. My accent is O.K. We are allowed to change the sequence of our lines. We may add something such as, "Write your name and address clearly on your suitcases," or invent some soothing comments. Ossi listens as we each pronounce our lines. When we are finished we listen to the music playing in our lounge. There are tunes from the film *Cabaret* (1972). Ossi tells us that that was the first big film on which he worked as a consultant and dialect coach. Probably everyone remembers the song, "Willkommen, bienvenue, welcome." It was Joel Grey, singing with a hard German accent as the unforgettable emcee in *Cabaret,* a part for which he earned an Oscar. His accent was the result of coaching by Ossi Ragheb, who also plays a small part as a border patrolman in *Schindler's List*. Now, possibly to relax us, he tells us stories about teaching American actors the nuances of proper pronunciation, such as the word *talented*. The emphasis is normally on the first syllable, but Ossi taught Joel Grey to accent the second-to-the-last syllable: tal•ent'•ed. After that lesson, a noted German actor approached Joel Grey, and speaking in English, told him that he was very "tal•ent'•ed." This was Ossi's triumphal moment.

We are called onto the set. We now belong to the assistant directors, who set up the preliminary sequence for filming. Marek has one idea and Sergio another. The final decision is Spielberg's. He just arrived in his cherry-colored Audi. For crowd scenes he is always accompanied by his personal bodyguard, Darek Ivański. Steven is greeting Liam Neeson and Beatrice Macola, playing his friend Ingrid.

Spielberg does not know that I am supposed to act today, and he raises his eyebrows when he sees me in my suit and fedora. Then he gives me a big smile, so I walk up to him.

"Today I am a German clerk."

"Wonderful," he answers, "but let me fix your hat." He takes my hat and rolls down the brim.

"Is it supposed to be more like Indiana Jones?" I ask.

"Yes. You know this is my expertise," he answers. Who wouldn't know? Right now Polish television is broadcasting *Chronicles of the Young Indiana Jones*.

Just then, Jerry Molen, Steven Spielberg's producer, arrives on the set.

"What's going on? Are you filming *Casablanca*?" he jokes.

'Well, of course you recognize Humphrey Bogart," I answer. Personally, I prefer to be compared to Humphrey Bogart—but I'd settle for Indiana Jones.

During my consultation with Spielberg, David James, the official still photographer, approaches and takes a souvenir photo of us. He has made still photos for 120 films, among them *Fiddler on the Roof* (1971), *Yentl* (1983), *Jesus Christ Superstar* (1973), *Battle of Britain* (1969), and the whole *Rambo* series (1982, 1985, 1988). He travels with film companies all over the world and knows everyone who is worth knowing in the film industry. He can talk for hours about meeting or conversing with such celebrities as Jack Nicholson, Marlon Brando, and others whose names would make one dizzy. His hobby is fly fishing.

Immediately after his arrival in Kraków he asked me where we could go fly fishing for trout. When the season opened we took him to the Dunajec River near Łopuszna, but unfortunately, by that time the snow had begun to melt in the Tatra Mountains and the heavy runoff caused the water to be high. He only caught one trout, which was undersize, but he took a bath up to his neck in the Dunajec several times. That evening, around the campfire drying out our clothes—drinking one bottle of vodka after another—the local *Górale** peasants were full of questions about his films.

---

*Górale are Polish folk living in the Carpathian Mountains in southern Poland. They speak a peasant dialect.

"Well, Mister, how many of those film things have you made?"

"One hundred and twenty," David says.

"How many years are on you?"

"Fifty," David answers.

"Well, to me it seems you must be a hundred and fifty 'cause when could you have had time to make all them films," was the conclusion.

It was as an egalitarian club of fly fisherman that we finally found grounds for an understanding, especially when David told them a story about the famous British actor Michael Hordern, who was knighted by Queen Elizabeth for his achievements. When asked what he considered his own great achievement, David related how Hardy, the famous rod-and-tackle firm, purchased a license for a fly that he had created and sold the fly for over a year. David's stories impressed the locals in Łopuszna on the Dunajec.

We must return from reminiscing about our excursion to the beautiful clear waters of the Dunajec River to the platform of Kraków Station, where Steven Spielberg is setting up for the next take. It is a hot day. We are not envious of the engineers in the locomotive as we were just two months ago in Birkenau. On the platform beside the locomotive there is a crowd of Jews with suitcases and satchels. My film partners Brian and Steven stay on the platform where they will repeat their three sentences through megaphones over the din of the crowd. Spielberg instructs me to stand before the entrance to the platform. In a moment a crowd of Jews who have been unloaded from trucks will come toward me. As they approach the platform I am supposed to say my lines, then Oskar Schindler arrives in a car. He will pass us and the camera will follow him to the platform, where he can see with his own eyes how the Jews are being deported to the concentration camps. At the moment Schindler passes me I am supposed to stop talking.

Spielberg walks up to me and gives me last-minute directions. He tells me which sentences I can use. I do not need to stick strictly to the text. My situation is better than actors like Branko Lustig, playing the maître d' in the restaurant. He has to repeat a take if he changes the word sequence.

Steven gives directions quietly, soothing the actor. I need it at this moment, though I have twenty years of experience in front of a TV camera and a year of studies at Columbia University in New York City. I have stage fright, feeling I have forgotten my English completely and will not be able to utter my three simple sentences correctly. I console myself that in the general hubbub perhaps anything goes.

Fat chance! A sound man arrives and installs a wireless mike on me. Now it is certain that nothing will be hidden from the ears of Ossi and Spielberg, who always wears earphones during filming and can hear everything. No hope that the sound man, Ron Judkins, will stick the plug in wrong. He is a first-class expert who worked with Spielberg on *Hook, Jurassic Park,* and *Arachnophobia,* among others, and on such other projects as *Dad* (1989), *Hero* (1992), *Toys* (1992), *Drugstore Cowboy* (1989), *Choose Me* (1989), *Trouble in Mind* (1985), *Made in Heaven* (1987), and *The Moderns* (1988). So nothing was left to do but concentrate "to the max" and try to act.

"Well, that's what you wanted, you dumbbell," I murmur to myself, again under my breath.

"Rehearsal!" yell the assistants through bullhorns. "Attention! ACTION!" A crowd of Jews is approaching, right at me. When am I supposed to start saying my lines? Hey, no one will tell me that now. Better now than later, I think, better that the sound man has more sounds to delete than if he has holes in the sound track. The Polish playwright Aleksander Fredro always believed it is easier to make something thin out of fat than to fatten something thin.

"Leave your belongings on the platform, leave it all here. Pay attention that all is well labeled. Write your name and address on your suitcases. Your luggage will follow you on your journey." I inform rather than shout, quietly, with persuasion, with reassurance, as Spielberg advised. I hear a command. "STOP! Return to position number one!" That means from the beginning. Spielberg wants "my" Jews to enter onto the platform and stop. I am to give them pieces of chalk, with which they will write their names on their suitcases. They should form a crowd, which Oskar Schindler will try to squeeze through. Ossi walks up to me and corrects my pronunciation of "labeled."

One more rehearsal, and then the command, "Attention, we are filming the take!" From behind the camera, I hear Steven's soft "Action!" The crowd is approaching. My nervousness has disappeared somewhere. "Leave your luggage on the platform. Make sure it is clearly labeled. Your luggage will follow you. Leave your luggage on the platform, leave it here." I distribute chalk to write names and addresses. I repeat the same lines once more. At that moment Oskar Schindler passes by me. This means my bit is finished. No—there is the sacramental command from Spielberg: "Excellent! We will do it once more!" We do. "Well, we have a take," Spielberg informs us. So, that's all? Or maybe, it's that much!

I look around at my newly-made friends and acquaintances. Steven Tate, an assistant camera operator, gives me a thumbs-up that everything went well. This feeling of mutual camaraderie and eagerness to help will not leave me as long as I am on the set. It is a good beginning, but still a long road to the end of the day. I do not participate in the next take. It is a scene involving loading the Jews onto the wagons. I have an opportunity to exchange some thoughts with Mietek Pemper.

During the war, Mietek Pemper was a stenographer for Amon Goeth. Through that job he had access to all kinds of secret information, which he conveyed to Oskar Schindler. Thanks to getting his name on Schindler's list he survived the war, and afterwards was a witness for the prosecution at the trial of Goeth. When liberation was imminent Schindler spoke briefly to "his" Jews before leaving Brinnlitz with a few selected Jews in order to escape to the American zone. A stenographic transcript of the speech exists and is quoted in full by Thomas Keneally in his book. (Keneally has just arrived in Kraków and has come to the set of *Schindler's List*.) Among other things, Oskar Schindler said, "Don't thank me for your survival. Thank your people who worked day and night to save you from extermination. Thank your fearless Stern and Pemper and a few others, who, thinking of you and worrying about you, especially in Kraków, have faced death every moment."

Mietek Pemper lives in Augsburg, Germany, and just came to Kraków for three days at Steven Spielberg's invitation to be the film's guest of honor. Here, at the freight-train station on Kamienna Street, the real Mietek Pemper and Ben Kingsley, the film Itzhak Stern, meet. It is to Pemper and Stern—men of selfless courage and daring—that so many people owe their lives.

Assured that I'm available, Zdravko Madsarevic, who checks attendance, permits me to sit in the shade of a weeping willow just breaking into foliage and talk with Mietek Pemper. I realize that what Pemper often sees on the location is quite different from the actual events that he lived through. Many surviving eyewitnesses dislike the fact that directors of documentaries do not film all the happenings as they actually occurred in real life. These witnesses are so attached to their memories it is difficult for them to understand that the truth of real life and the truth seen on the screen are two different matters. Mietek Pemper belongs to those who understand that their lives have become public property. He does not intend to control the creativity of the director with minute details. "I am here to help, if needed, and not to interfere," he answers my question about his personal perception of what he sees on the set.

I want to verify with Pemper something I learned from Janina Olszewska, which concerns the scene presently being filmed. According to Janina, Oskar Schindler pulled Bankier, the former co-owner of Emalia, out of the deportation train and not Itzhak Stern, as described in the Keneally book and in the movie script. Mietek Pemper concurs with Janina, but in the film Bankier is not even mentioned. Also in the film, the part of Mietek is reduced to a nonspeaking episode. As created by Ben Kingsley, the character of Itzhak Stern is actually a composite of three persons: Stern, Bankier, and Mietek Pemper.

Unfortunately, we do not have time for a long conversation. An assistant to the director calls me on the set. In the next take Brian, Steven, and myself are supposed to stand on the train platform to serve as background for Oskar Schindler's conversation with Tauber, a clerk from the Gestapo, and a German sergeant, Kunder. Kunder is played by Grzegorz Damięcki and the Gestapo clerk by Joachim Paul Schultze, from Vienna. Schindler finds out that Stern is on the transport, but he is also on Tauber's transport list, so a mistake is out of the question. Schindler offers both officials the promise of arranging a trip for them to the Russian front.

In addition to me and my two companions serving as background, there are the faces and hands of Jews seen through the jagged networks of barbed wire that cover the "windows" of the cattle wagons. During the pauses between the consecutive run-throughs, the assistants call for more faces and hands in the windows; the extras better do more than a little arm-waving to earn their daily keep. More windows than just those closest to the camera must be filled with active hands and faces. In the window just behind Schindler there are two American friends of Brian and Steven, a young man and woman who also signed up to be extras in Spielberg's film. After a few run-throughs, Spielberg "buys" the take.

Then the next scene begins as all three—Schindler, Kunder, and Gestapo clerk Tauber—walk briskly alongside the train calling out Stern's name to find the wagon he is in. At that moment the train is starting to move. The Gestapo clerk jumps onto the locomotive to stop it. Obviously the idea of a trip to the Russian front does not appeal to him. When this shot is finished, we break for lunch.

Lunch is served from a canteen vehicle next to a large tent with tables and benches. Usually there are two meat dishes. The vegetarians can gorge themselves from a great variety of cooked vegetables, salads, and fruit set up on a table inside the tent. One line is just to serve the actors and crew; the extras are served in a separate line. Because the crew consists of over fifty people, a certain hierarchy is observed. The camera crew is served first. I am surprised to find out that actors in a small episode like mine also receive priority treatment. I take my place behind Ralph Fiennes, who does not act today, but showed up on the set in his jeans and a T-shirt. After a while, a waiter walks up to me and invites me to stand at the head of the line. I protest and point to Ralph—the star should be ahead of me—but they both explain that I have priority seating because this is my working day. My embarrassment vanishes moments later when I notice that Ralph, too, is pulled out of the line. How wonderful it is to be a star.

After lunch we rest in the Club bus. Soon our intoxicating time of being in the company of stars from Spielberg's film is interrupted by a call from an assistant: The director is already on the set and arranging the next shot. Now the camera is installed inside the cab of the locomotive. The filming of the Gestapo Tauber jumping into the cab will be done from the interior of the locomotive. Though the speed of the starting train is very slow, Spielberg asks the actor to be especially cautious. Our trio takes the same place as in the previous scene. Though we serve only as background, we have to be in the identical position as before. This is very important, so that when the director is editing he is free to blend and arrange pictorial elements to his liking. If our position is not the same, the individual fragments have to be "animated," in film lingo. An ordinary movie viewer would probably not notice it, but a professional will always see the discrepancies.

The editor for *Schindler's List* is Michael Kahn, one of the leading professionals in the field, who also has stopped in Kraków for a few days. He has worked with Spielberg for many

years. Their cooperative efforts earned a Best Editing Oscar for
Raiders of the Lost Ark (1981) and Oscar nominations for *Close
Encounters of the Third Kind* (1977) and *Empire of the Sun* (1987).
Michael also edited other films for Spielberg: *Hook* (1991),
Indiana Jones and the Temple of Doom (1984), *Indiana Jones and the
Last Crusade* (1989), *The Color Purple* (1985), and *Poltergeist*
(1982).

Kraków is becoming a town where Hollywood celebrities drop
in just for the weekend. A week after George Lucas came to
Kraków, Sidney J. Sheinberg, head of Universal Pictures, arrives with Tom Pollack, head of film production at Universal.
They spend Sunday sightseeing in the city and drinking coffee
in Jama Michalika, the popular elegant cafe. For two days now
they have been on Spielberg's set at the freight station on
Kamienna Street. Sidney J. Sheinberg was the "matchmaker" in
starting the production of *Schindler's List* because he was the one
to call Steven Spielberg's attention to Thomas Keneally's book.
He should also be credited with the discovery of Steven
Spielberg, having signed his first contract.

It all started in 1965 during an excursion by a group of high
school students to Los Angeles. Universal Pictures was on the
itinerary. Seventeen-year-old Steven Spielberg broke away from
the group and decided to see the film production process from
the ground up, not just via the routine tourist trail. Somehow he
got into no less than the office of the head of editing, Chuck
Silvers, who, instead of calling a guard to throw out the
intruder, talked with him for an hour. As they said goodbye,
Silvers said he would like to see samples of Spielberg's films.
Armed with a pass, Spielberg visited Universal all through the
summer. The guards, without question, let in the young man
dressed in a suit and carrying a borrowed briefcase, taking him
for a son of one of the Universal executives. Spielberg mingled
with directors, scenographers, and editors, but with no results.
One day he found an empty room in which he decided to make

a nest for himself. He went to a store, where he bought some plastic letters, and on the board of the building directory placed information about his "office": Steven Spielberg, Room 22 C.

After graduation from high school, the following fall Spielberg entered California State College at Long Beach.* His application to study film at UCLA had not met with success. Of course, he wanted to study film at Long Beach as well, but ended up in English. He had many kinds of part-time jobs to finance production of his films, then in 16mm format. Later he got a job at Universal for three days a week. At last he had the opportunity to study the work of the great artists—among them Alfred Hitchcock. One day, however, an assistant to the director threw him off the set of the film *Torn Curtain*.

Stephen's determination was enormous. A wealthy school friend who dreamed of becoming a film producer put up $10,000, and Steven made a twenty-two-minute film titled *Amblin'* (1969). It is a simple film, without dialogue, about a boy and a girl hitchhiking through the desert to the Pacific Ocean. Production of the film lasted ten days. The camera operator was Allan Daviau, who later became cinematographer for *E.T.* The day after screening, Spielberg was called before Sidney J. Sheinberg, then head of television production at Universal. *Amblin'* made such a great impression on Sheinberg that he offered the twenty-one-year old Spielberg a seven-year contract with Universal Pictures. Though Steven was afraid of how his parents would react to the news of an interruption in his college education, he immediately accepted the offer and jumped right into the stream of work—so quickly, he says, that he did not have time to clean up his affairs at the college. *Amblin'* received an award at the film festival in Atlanta and at the 1969 Venice festival. The title of this lucky-for-Spielberg film became the name of his own film studio. The future would later show that the seven-year contract given Spielberg was Sheinberg's hap-

---

*The California State College at Long Beach became a university in June 1972, six years after Steven Spielberg enrolled.

piest hiring decision, one which brought hundreds of millions of dollars into Universal's coffers.

After lunch with all the "dignitaries" we continue filming our scene. This will be the sixteenth take of scene 95. Each is repeated several times. In the previous takes Oskar Schindler, running alongside the barbed-wired wagons, finally found the one with Itzhak Stern. After the train stops, Stern will be dragged out of the wagon. Schindler will sign some papers and they will both return to the factory.

It is late in the afternoon when Ben Kingsley enters the set, though he was available from early in the morning in case the director needed him. Kingsley enters a cattle wagon. The camera is placed on a dolly which will be pulled backward about three hundred feet. During that time Stern will be explaining to Schindler how it happened that he could have been sent away with a transport. This take is long, it lasts about a minute, but a lot is happening and it includes dialogue. We begin a rehearsal. The train stops with a loud jar and a cloud of steam, and Sergeant Kunder orders the soldiers on the platform to open the wagon. Stern falls out onto the platform. Schindler hurries toward the exit. Stern follows him and struggles to put on a coat. Tauber also runs after Schindler, thrusting some papers at him to sign. Tauber explains that his papers must be in order even if the man on the transport is different. Then just the two, Schindler and Stern, proceed toward the exit speaking their lines as the train again begins to move slowly, leaving the station with the transport to the death camp.

From this condensed description it is evident that there is a lot of action, many people, and a locomotive which brakes and then starts again. The director wants the scene to be really dynamic. Maciek, one of the assistants to the director, armed with a radio telephone, sits next to the engineer in the locomotive, and after more than twelve tries to start, slow down, brake, stop, back up, and start again could pass an examination for an engineer or an assistant engineer for sure. After a few rehearsals Steven himself sits behind the camera. Doubtless, he remembers the saying that the true creator of the film is the one who sits behind the viewfinder of the camera. The first rehearsal of that take is interrupted by Steven after a few seconds. He wants the group of soldiers who are to open the wagon to start closer to the camera. During the second try, which he also interrupts, he tells them to run faster toward the wagon. Then Liam, as Schindler, while signing the papers for Tauber, lifts the pages too high, covering his face. During the following try Tauber, hastily following Schindler, is swinging his hips, which Spielberg does not like. Then Ben Kingsley can't get his arm into his sleeve and struggles too much with his coat. Liam has some problems with the text— and so on and so on. I take a look at the clapboard on which the secretary writes the consecutive takes: Q, scene: 95. When the number of run-throughs reaches ten, Brian, Steven, and I start to take bets. I bet on thirteen. It turns out I was an optimist.

The ending of the scene is played at one end of the platform about fifty feet from us, so we do not hear Steven's remarks. We see only that Liam Neeson is going in our direction into position number one, so we jokingly repeat Stephen's customary remark, "That was wonderful. Let's repeat it one more time." And we do.

Steven wants a short break. Liam Neeson and Ben Kingsley sit down in their chairs for a moment. The doors of the wagons are opened to let in some fresh air. The extras leave the wagons and walk up to the stars, asking for autographs. The most common papers which Liam Neeson and Ben Kingsley auto-graphed were 1,000 złoty bills [10 American cents]*—which

---

*The 1,000-złoty note mentioned here is of the so-called old money. By 1993 the value of the złoty had so diminished with inflation that the Polish government announced its intention to drop the last four zeros from all of its money. The 1,000-złoty note used for autographs would be worth 1/10 of one of today's złoty. Because the 1,000-złoty note was known to be headed for extinction, using them as the company members did would be linking a rare signature with a soon-to-be rare specimen of the old Polish currency. The value of 1,000 old złoty in 1993 was about 10 American cents; today it is worth about 3 cents— without the autograph.

may have given Spielberg an idea for enriching the scene just filmed.

In the next run-through he tells extras in the wagons to hand secret notes through the barred windows to Ben Kingsley as he is leaving the wagon. Spielberg places Steven (from our trio) next to the wagon and tells him to take the notes away from Kingsley and tear them up. Kingsley likes such surprises. During the discussion session after the *Gandhi* screening at the Wanda movie theater, he spoke about Spielberg:

> He is a wonderful human being and a highly creative one. He has so many dynamic, new ideas. On one hand, he has a vision for his film and he knows what he wants to accomplish. On the other hand, he loves to concentrate on details—on the particular film fragment he is working through at a given moment. He changes the dialogue or the action of the scene many times in order to achieve the best effect. I love this kind of spontaneity, this mode of work because it forces one to engage all one's energy. I think that since working with Richard Attenborough on *Gandhi,* Spielberg is the next director with whom I have collaborated that can combine vision with the everyday toil of filmmaking.

What we are presently doing is the best example of Ben Kingsley's thesis. First run-through, second, third. Finally, after the seventeenth, we hear, "We have a take." There is only one thing left to be filmed. The camera focuses on all the clerks and soldiers, who are leaving the platform after a job well done, then shifts to the heap of signed suitcases. My partners, Brian and Steven, and I had told the people to leave them behind on the platform and they—supposedly—would follow later. Our victims never saw their suitcases again.

I also want to have a souvenir of the day I worked close to the stars Liam Neeson and Ben Kingsley. True, I see them every day, and thanks to my friends Poldek and Mila Page and Niusia Karakulska, they treat me differently than just another worker serving on the set—but to be their partner on the set, that's another story. I take the script I was given that morning and walk over to both of them. Saying that my day's experience in the film is probably my first and last, I ask them to commemorate the day with their autographs. Liam Neeson writes, "Greetings and Congratulations"; Ben Kingsley, "Best Wishes."

Before I returned home, I had to sign a document consisting of three pages in the form of a contract. It read, in effect, that between Heritage Films—the management of production for the film *Schindler's List,* located in Warsaw, also known as the Producer in the name and interest for which they are working, the Chairman of Management, Lew Rywin, and Director of Production Michał Szczerbic, and Mr. Franciszek Palowski, called according to the agreement an Actor, an agreement was reached accordingly:

> The Producer gives the Actor and the Actor is obliged to perform the part of a Civilian Clerk (English-speaking), in the film directed by the director Steven Spielberg under the title *Schindler's List* according to the script given to the Actor in the English-language version and according to the agreement between the Actor and the Director during the filming from 04/26/1993 to 05/29/1993 under the terms agreed upon with the Producer. In addition, the Actor agrees to participate in the fittings of costumes, rehearsal for makeup, lessons in English pronunciation, and also participate in the process of postsynchronization within the stated time frame.

This is, of course, only the first paragraph of a three-page document.

After returning home around 8:00 P.M. (the work day lasted

thirteen hours), I asked my wife not to forget to place a copy of the contract in my coffin. In the end, one never knows what this "widow's penny" may weigh at the Last Judgment.

"You have told me to put so many things into your coffin there will not be any room for you," she remarked.

11

The Order of the Smile

On Sunday, May 23, the Television Studio for Production of Art Programs in Łęg near Kraków gathered several hundred children from all over Poland. They all were admirers of E.T.— Extra Terrestrial—and his creator, Steven Spielberg. *E.T. The Extra Terrestrial* (1982) woke up the imagination and feelings of hundreds of millions of people around the world. Though Spielberg has directed many wonderful films, grownups and children alike still love him because he created that deeply humanistic film about the necessity of loving a strange creature not of this earth. The gathering was organized for the purpose of awarding the director the highest recognition that the Polish children had at their disposal—the Order of the Smile. Though Steven Spielberg was terribly busy directing and editing his film, the crowd in Łęg had hopes that he would break away from work for a while and show up unexpectedly, just as E.T. did.

It all began with a visit by Janusz Zaorski, the head of Polish Radio and Television, to the set of the Płaszów camp in the Liban quarry. The crew had just finished shooting the scene depicting the execution by hanging of Amon Goeth, the commandant of the Płaszów camp. The day before I had made many calls to law professors at Jagiellonian University attempting to find out how that gruesome ceremony might have looked. Of course, no one in the company had ever seen a hanging. It was enormously important that our version sustain the authenticity of the rest of the film. About midnight, the producer, Branko Lustig, also called me about the matter of the execution. Everybody seemed to be upset, but the next day, exactly at noon, we hanged Amon Goeth. It was a cruel and very realistically enacted scene that Ralph Fiennes played. There was absolute silence around the set, though everyone knew that it was only acting. It was immediately after that, as if in counterpoint to the scene, that Zaorski announced the plan for awarding the Order of the Smile to Spielberg. Everybody was invited to attend the ceremony in the Łęg studio two weeks later.

Right up to the last day no one was certain if Steven would show up. Anything could be expected to happen in the last two days of filming. For example, if the weather forecast was bad, the producers might have to schedule additional time for shooting on Sunday. On Friday morning Jerry Molen informed Lew Rywin that Spielberg's participation in the ceremony was out of the question, but that afternoon, after hearing another series of arguments for accepting the invitation, Jerry told me that Steven would show up. He would not come for the presentation of the whole show prepared by the children, however, just for the presentation of the award. It was possible that he would even stay for only a few extra minutes. With the director of the celebration, Krzysztof Jasiński, we worked out the precise moment in the spectacle's scenario for staging the ceremony awarding the Order of the Smile.

Noon, exactly, the whole auditorium in Łęg was filled to capacity. The introductory warm-up for the program, which was to be recorded in its entirety, began. Grażyna Torbicka and Charles Poe arrived in the studio on an old motorcycle. Charles was costumed as Indiana Jones, the most popular of Spielberg's characters after E.T.

Poe, an American living in Kraków, is a newsman on radio RMF and a coworker on Spielberg's film, who helped Ossi

Ragheb in coaching the actors for *Schindler's List* in proper
American pronunciation. Poe came to the Łęg studio in order to
express appreciation on behalf of ordinary Americans for
bestowing the Order of the Smile on Spielberg.

The entire program was broadcast in English, which was only
logical, because how could one communicate with E.T. other-
wise, or with Steven Spielberg if he happened to arrive in Łęg.
Therefore, all the children invited to participate had studied
English.

The entertainment lasted for forty-five minutes. Among
other stories, they presented the history of the Wawel Dragon,*
somewhat modernized to feature E.T., who this time does not
land in a small American town, but in Kraków. Furthermore, it
happened a long time ago when the horrible and hungry dragon
lived. E.T. is given a friendly greeting by the people of Kraków.
But the dragon, well, that's another story. Everybody knows
about the horribly frightening dragon that lives in a cave under
Wawel Castle; his fiery breath keeps ordinary people at a
distance. The stranger doesn't know, though. The dragon asks
the strange visitor for its name. E.T. says, "Let's be friends, I am
E.T." The dragon knows very little English but knows the word
EaT. Anyway, the dragon is always hungry and he interprets
everything as food. So, of course, he gobbles up E.T.—but that's
not the end of the story. Stories such as this have to have happy

---

*The Wawel Dragon, named Baziliszek, is a major legendary
symbol in Kraków. Wawel is the medieval-renaissance castle and
battlements established on a promontory above the Wisła River not far
from Rynek Główny, the old town square. Wawel was the residence of
ancient kings, such as King Kazimierz the Great, King Zygmunt the
Old, and King Zygmunt August. Legend has it that the dragon lived in
caves under Wawel Castle. Today when one visits the castle, one can
visit the dragon's cave, scrambling down an exciting underground
system of walks, steps, and caves to an exit below on the bank of the
Wisła River. There, outside the lower mouth of the cave, is a giant iron
sculpture of the craggy dragon. Flame spews from its mouth
periodically, courtesy of the local gas company.

endings. It turns out that E.T. is not "EaTable." Instead, he gives the dragon a bad case of indigestion. The dragon's belly bursts open and E.T. comes out to play with the children of Kraków.

Well, no sooner was the dragon taken care of than Branko Lustig brought word that Steven Spielberg was arriving momentarily. Branko was amazed at the number of children present. Even in the Hollywood studios one would not find that many children, he said.

At 1:15 P.M. Steven Spielberg arrives. So, he did come, though no one had been certain until the last minute. During his three month's stay in Kraków he refused many meetings, but evidently he did not want to disappoint the children. Spielberg shot many scenes of his recent film in the same studio in which he now meets the children. The scenography is new. Marek Grabowski is in charge, using elements from Spielberg's and George Lucas's films incorporated with the local traditions of Kraków. Spielberg is surprised and probably a bit taken by the warm reception.

The most important moment of the whole program—the ceremony of bestowing the Order of the Smile—is approaching. The event can never be repeated.

"Is Mr. Spielberg present?" the leader of the chapter of the Order of the Smile asks.

"Present."

"Please approach." The Order is pinned on and the proclamation is read.

"In the name of the chapter of the Order of the Smile I have the honor to name you Knight of the Order of the Smile—the most joyful Order in the world. The leader dubs the new knight using the traditional long-stemmed red rose.

After that, Spielberg is sworn in: that he will always be full of joy and will strive to bring joy and happiness to all the children in the world. Well, it was easy to take an oath, but has he enough self-denial to keep his word? He has to prove it in public by drinking a whole glass of lemon juice without sugar, and in addition he has to smile afterwards—oh yes! This is not a joke. This is quite different from directing a film—but he comes out of the test with dignity; he smiles and says that never in this life has he tasted such delicious lemonade!

Now there is opportunity for a brief conversation. Karoline is to begin; she has had some experience in this matter. When she previously came with her friend to visit the set she met Steven and interviewed him briefly, so now she has the right to ask the first question:

"What would you do if suddenly E.T. landed in the backyard of your home?"

"I think I would not hide him from others like the hero of my film did; I would share this joyful occasion with everyone," Steven answers.

When Ania asks which was his most difficult film to produce, the answer was *Raiders of the Lost Ark*. Ania is curious what he wanted to be when he was a child. Steven answers that ever since he was eleven years old he always dreamed of becoming a film director—and he did everything he could to make his dream come true.

Dominika wants to know if children act in all his films. Steven cannot recall a film of his without children.

Then Karoline asks if he will continue producing films for children.

"Oh yes," Steven answers, "just like one of my greatest idols, Walt Disney, who devoted his life to the production of films for children."

When someone asks, "Will you continue making films like *E.T.* or *Close Encounters*?" Spielberg answers that he seeks new inspiration continuously.

"Do you love Polish children?"

"Of course," is Steven's immediate reply. "In *Schindler's List*, which is not a film for children, there are only Polish children and they are excellent actors. Besides, I came here with my own children, who made a lot of friends in Poland, and," he adds, "working on this film was a great experience." He explains that just last evening during a banquet celebrating the conclusion of filming for *Schindler's List,* he had compared the work on this film to a road. "Today I can say that, in the end, this was the most significant road in my life."

To end the event in Łęg, Steven is shown a short medley of dances depicting all of Kraków's legends. Maybe this will be an inspiration for his next film for children, because E.T. was watching it all. At one point during a lively Krakovian dance, girls in traditional Krakovian costumes pull Spielberg into the dance line. Later, one of the girls brags that Steven knelt in front of her as part of the dance—and did it very gracefully. I do not know if during the swirling dancing of the Krakówiak some of Steven's Polish Jewish Galician ancestral roots were awakened, or if it was just the child in his soul—like the one buried deep in each of us, but there is no doubt that Steven can be happy and joyous, like a child. As he leaves, he expresses his pleasure at having experienced such an unexpectedly splendid reception: "Deep in my heart I carry the experience of the past three-and-a-half months. This is a wonderful country, where people are warm, friendly, and generous, to me as well as to my actors, of whom many are Polish. I'll be back for sure, maybe to make another film," he adds. Everybody wants his autograph.

He probably would never have been able to leave the studio if his coworkers had not come to the rescue.

The next day, during filming of a segment in Bonarka, he sports the Order of the Smile, pinned to his chest. When I speak with him, he tells me that he will always wear it. That day, one of the last scenes in *Schindler's List* is filmed—the liberation from Brinnlitz: The gate to Oskar Schindler's factory is open. A Russian officer rides up on a small horse, stops a few meters before the gate and proclaims to the Schindler Jews, "You have been liberated by the Red Army." The Jews were already free people; they were liberated earlier, thanks to guns Schindler bought on the black market.

The small horse is loaded with bags of goods; the soldier's chest is decorated with golden medals. Only he and Steven Spielberg are decorated that day, but Spielberg's Order is the greatest symbol of lasting peace.

The last hours of filming *Schindler's List* in Kraków. It rained the night before and the producers are worried about the schedule for the next two days. There cannot be any delays or accidents. The company is booked to fly to Israel on Thursday. Luckily, after the all-night rain and morning fog, sunshine returns. The last scene is filmed in Bonarka in the old factory belonging to the Active Society for Chemical Industry, "Liban."

Evening. Fragments of the inactive factory are illuminated by large reflectors. This is to be the scene of Oskar Schindler's and his wife's departure to the American zone, escorted by a few Schindler Jews from Brinnlitz. Standing next to his car, Schindler says goodbye to Itzhak Stern. They are surrounded by a few hundred extras.

It is late and everybody is tired. The closer to the end of filming, the longer every minute seems to last. Every additional request by the director is regarded as simply a whim. He could put together four *Schindler's Lists* from the two hundred fifty thousand feet of film shot up until now.

More people than usual are on the set. Besides those working on the film, there are their friends and acquaintances. There, too, is Robert Bawol, the man who was saved by the Szewczyk family during the war.

There is a solemn mood during the last hours of filming. Spielberg has just been informed that they have reached over two thousand takes. In such moments one can observe the true nature of Spielberg—he demands the ultimate effort from himself as well as from others up to the very end.

It is 2:00 A.M., Wednesday. Nearby, in a small swamp, one can hear the frogs croaking. Lew Rywin says that at this time it is silly to go the bed; in an hour one can go fishing. He's been dreaming for a long time now of those fish in the Mazury Lake country.

2:10 A.M. Spielberg says, "Wrap!"

Applause, champagne corks pop. Everybody congratulates everybody. Flowers for the director from the extras. I see a strange reflection in Steven's eyes—tears? Later I ask several others if they noticed it too.

"Yes."

Then someone adds, "I've worked in film for thirty-three years, but I have never seen a director so moved after the last take."

12

Schindler's Ark

Steven Spielberg decided to film the last scene of *Schindler's List* in Jerusalem, at the Catholic Cemetery located on the slopes of Mt. Zion where Oskar Schindler was buried in 1974. The idea was conceived in Kraków but was not included in all the changes in the script. Back around the middle of April, during a visit to the set by Poldek Page, the idea must have already existed in the Spielberg imagination because Poldek and Anna Maria Stein made a list of people whom Steven Spielberg wanted to invite to Jerusalem, verifying addresses and telephone numbers. Of course, it was not to be a reunion of all the Schindler Jews, who are living all over the world and at present number about six thousand people, counting their children and grandchildren. That's a bigger number than all the Jews living in Poland today.* The invitations to Jerusalem were issued only to those whose names were mentioned in the book and were included in the script. The actors who portrayed them in the film were also to travel to Jerusalem.

When Poldek was leaving for Los Angeles and saying good-bye to Spielberg, he pointed at me and said, "Steven, I would like this gentleman to fly to Israel, too. If necessary I'll cover the

---

*In 1939, there were three million Jews living in Poland; today there are fewer than six thousand.

cost of his trip." The next morning Jerry Molen told me that I was included in his list of participants. In addition, I would be a guide, interpreter, and caretaker. Thus, I became a member of the group which was to fly on the charter plane.

On Thursday, May 27, at 8:00 A.M. a LOT airplane piloted by Captain Andrzej Salamon took off from the Balice Airport with seventy passengers. Among them was Liam Neeson, Caroline Goodall, Beatrice Macola, and all the Israeli actors returning home: Jonathan Sagalle, Schmulik Levy, Mark Ivanir, Embeth Davidtz, Adi Nitzan, Miri Fabian, and Ezra Dagan. Traveling along with the adult Polish actors and Kraków children was Kroke, a group of musicians who performed Jewish music at the Ariel coffee house on Szeroka Street. For many days the coffeehouse was an informal club for the participants in *Schindler's List*. During the flight, Jacek Wójcicki, who portrayed the violinist Rosner, disappeared into the cockpit, and later, in his inimitable sprightly cabaret persona, assured us it was really he who piloted the plane. Also flying with us was a cantor, Włodzimierz Kamiński.

Włodzimierz Kamiński worked on *Schindler's List* as a consultant for Jewish religious matters—after all, someone had to instruct the Polish actors how to pray on the Sabbath and how to perform a wedding ceremony. He was also included as an actor in two episodes. Actually, Kamiński's life story could also be the basis for a sensational film. He is a Ukrainian Jew, and when the war started he was a second-year student in medical school. He was one of the first to be drafted into the Red Army, but during the battle at Poltava the German Army took him prisoner. As a Jew and an officer in the Red Army, he had no chance of surviving German capture. What to do? His ID documents were easily destroyed, but his circumcision was a different matter. Włodzimierz dreamed up a new identity. "I am a Muslim from the Caucasus Mountains," he told the commission who interrogated him. "My name is Emir Al Husein."

Nota bene: the producers of *Schindler's List* used their knowledge of this scheme when Spielberg demanded about fifty circumcised extras for a scene in the Płaszów camp. First they thought that Spielberg was joking by making such demands, but then it turned out that it was not a joke, that he *had to* have circumcised extras. The producers searched the refugee camps in Poland for Muslims from Bosnia, who according to customs similar to those of the Jews have to be circumcised before the age of thirteen. They finally found fifty volunteers willing to play the scene.

Włodzimierz Kamiński was successful in his deception. The Germans were more lenient toward the Caucasian nations, especially the Caucasus mountain folk, whom they found they could easily control, exercising the principle of divide and conquer. Włodzimierz learned some Arabic and Turkish, knew the Muslim prayers, and prayed to Allah every day. To kneel for devotions he used a burlap sack instead of a prayer rug. After a time as a prisoner in a camp at Żytomierz, he was put on a transport with other prisoners, but he managed to escape on the way to Olsztyn. A Polish peasant rescued him by providing a hiding place. A few years later he married the peasant's daughter, and so a Ukrainian Jew pretending to be a Muslim from the Caucasus ended up in Kraków. I was sitting next to him on the plane and was curious as to what he feared most as a German prisoner.

"That I would talk Hebrew in my sleep," he answered, "and someone would hear it. After all, we cannot control our dreams."

Włodzimierz Kamiński is an Ashkenazic Jew. Next to us was Ezra Dagan—a Sephardic Jew playing Rabbi Menasha Levartow in the film.* Levartow was a prominent intellectual and a scholar of the Talmud. The Kraków Jews therefore asked Oskar

---

*Ashkenazic Jews are those from Germany, Poland, and Russia, as distinguished from the Sephardic Jews, who are originally Spanish-Portuguese. The differences that arise from their diverse heritages are typically regarded as so extreme that any accord between them is often the basis for a bit of humorous reflection.

Schindler to place Levartow on his list; he was not an exceptional laborer, but definitely an exceptional human being. After the war he lived in New York City. One day he went for a walk with one of his students, who got distracted and was about to be hit by a passing car. In a second, Levartow jumped and pushed the student onto the sidewalk. The student was saved but Levartow was run over and killed.

There are various religious differences between the Sephardic and the Ashkenazic Jews, but Włodzimierz Kamiński and Ezra Dagan found a common prayer which they wanted to say together at the Catholic grave of Oskar Schindler in Jerusalem.

The three-hour flight over Ukraine, Romania, Istanbul, and Cyprus seemed but a moment. At the airport in Tel Aviv we were greeted by very hot weather. Even the black soldiers from Ghana—members of the United Nations contingent serving a peace mission in the Golan Heights—were seeking out the shade of palm trees. As we approached Jerusalem, the temperature became more moderate because the Holy City is over two hundred feet above the sea level. There was a cool breeze—ideal weather for sightseeing. I walked immediately to the Old City, whose walls I could see from the window of my room at the beautiful King David Hotel, where all the guests from *Schindler's List* were staying. This was my first encounter with the places I knew only from lectures but dreamed to visit: the Damascus Gate, the Tower of David, the Church of the Holy Sepulcher, the Via Dolorosa, the Ecce Homo Arch, the Mount of Olives, the Wailing Wall. As we entered the square at the Wailing Wall, an Israeli guard shot an Arab woman who had attacked him with a knife. A bullet also hit a five-months pregnant Jewish woman who was waiting to pray at the part of the wall reserved for women and separated from the men's part by a fence. The police cleared the square, but I had become witness to another fact about Jerusalem: the "City of Peace" is still only an ideal, though that ideal has been pursued for more than twenty centuries.

In the evening there was a gathering of the Schindler Jews, their actor counterparts, and Steven Spielberg in the banquet hall of the King David Hotel. About three hundred of them arrived from many parts of the world. There were married couples, such as Poldek and Mila Page, Henry and Mancy Rosner, Edzia and Sam Wertheim, and many others, who came from the United States, Argentina, Brazil, Australia. Many live in Israel. From Poland there was Niusia Horowitz-Karakulska and Stella Müller-Madej. People were telling each other from which street or town they came: Grodzka, Stradom, Nowy Sącz, Krynica. Emilie, the wife of Oskar Schindler, came from Argentina. She is an old lady, but one could still recognize her former beauty. She was sitting next to Marta, a close friend of Schindler through whom the Schindler Jews helped Oskar after the war by sending him money every month. Marta was not able to come to Kraków during the filming because her husband Bernard, also a former prisoner in the Płaszów camp, had an eye operation. Bernard, a specialist in building bridges, did not make the Schindler list because he was needed in Płaszów—first to build the camp and then to liquidate it. After he left Płaszów he was in four concentration camps; later he met and subsequently married Marta. Marta and Bernard escorted Emilie to Israel. After the long flight from Argentina, Emilie had stopped in New York for a short visit at Marta's home before they came on together to Jerusalem.

Steven Spielberg spoke to the guests and emphasized that this film was of great importance to him. Then he circulated from table to table, greeting everybody personally, posing for photos, and giving autographs. He worked like that without a pause for two hours. He did not have time to taste the delicious food especially prepared by the King David Hotel kitchen. Finally, he made his way to the table occupied by the Rosners. All of a sudden there was a different mood—sparks were flying—Leo Rosner had brought his accordion from Australia and started to play songs from before the war made popular by the famous Polish chanteuse, Ordonka. People had tears in their eyes. When

Jacek Wójcicki finally intoned "That Last Sunday," everybody joined in singing, gathering around the Rosners. A woman standing on a chair said to me, "I cannot believe it, what I am seeing. This must be something Oskar Schindler is arranging."

The management of the restaurant dimmed the lights several times to signal discreetly that the time allotted for the reception had passed, but still there was so much to tell, to listen to. We moved to the cafe on the terrace, though it was time to retire to our rooms. Tomorrow would be another day of filming—the busses would leave the hotel at 7:30 A.M.

I once saw a documentary film made during the Schindler funeral by Israeli TV. The procession began with Catholic priests, then a group of rabbis, and the Schindler Jews followed immediately after the coffin. The cemetery where Schindler rests is under the care of a nearby cloister of Franciscan brothers, five of whom it happens are of Polish descent. This place of final repose is located on Mount Zion outside the walls of the Old City but still very close to the most holy Christian places in Jerusalem: a ten-minute walk to the site of the Last Supper; nearby is the house of the Jewish high priest, Caiaphas, where Peter denied Christ, and the Church of the Dormition. Immediately behind the wall of the cemetery is an uninhabited valley overgrown by olive trees. This is the Hinnom Valley—*Ge-Hinnom* in Hebrew—meaning *Gehenna* or "hell." In ancient times an altar devoted to the Ammon tribal god Moloch stood here. Children were sacrificed by being burned on the altar. On the other side of the Hinnom Valley is the Mount of Evil Counsel, where the country home of Caiaphas was situated. On the left of the cemetery, at the bottom where the Hinnom Valley crosses the Cedron Valley, is Hakeldama, the Field of Blood, which tradition holds was bought by the archpriests for thirty shekels and reserved for the burial of foreigners who died in Jerusalem.

Today, the Hill of Evil Counsel is built up with ordinary homes. I could see a school and in a nearby field some boys were playing basketball. Ruins of old structures and some caves dot the Hinnom Valley. There are steps to one of the caves. These are ancient Jewish graves similar to that in which Christ was placed, and in which hermits lived in the Middle Ages. The valley is wild and beautiful. I was taking many photos from all sides when suddenly I felt I was looking at a scene right out of the Bible: a small herd of black or brown goats was running down into the Hinnom Valley and a herdsman in an Arab burnoose riding a white donkey joggled along after.

It is 8:00 A.M. Friday, May 23, 1993. Jerusalem. The Catholic Cemetery is slowly filling with the actors and their real-life counterparts from the last scene of Steven Spielberg's film. The grounds are bare. There are no trees except for some large cypresses by the wall bordering the Hinnom Valley. One dried-up cypress has fallen over. In the cemetery I find a few graves with Polish names. Judging from the dates, they must be General Anders's soldiers who were passing through from the Russian encampments at Monte Cassino, where the Allies and the Germans fought so bitterly from January to May 1944.*

The Oskar Schindler tomb is not far from the entrance to the

---

*A bit of history will help. When Hitler attacked Russia in 1941, General Anders organized Polish men, who had been sent to Russian gulags, into military units. Under an agreement made with the exile Polish government in London, they left Russia for Iran, going from Iran to Palestine, to Egypt, and finally to Italy. There, as part of the Allied forces, they participated in the Italian campaign. In 1944 there was a famous battle that resulted in the capture of the Benedictine monastery of Monte Cassino, located between Naples and Rome. During their military travels, many of these Polish soldiers died, some in Iran, others in Jerusalem, and so on, from the effects of hunger and disease experienced in the gulags. That is why we find some of their graves in Jerusalem.

cemetery. One has to walk along the wall of the catacombs and go down a few steps. On the cover of the tomb is an inscription: "Here rests Oskar Schindler, who saved 1,200 Jews during the Holocaust."

Spielberg sets up a camera next to the tomb. Those saved by Schindler and the actors portraying them will pass by. Spielberg's crew is reduced to a minimum: only one camera, with Janusz Kamiński, Raymond Stella, and Steve Tate; soundman Ron Judkins; makeup artist Christine Smith; and costume designer Anna Biedrzycka-Sheppard. There are only a few screens shading the location from too much sunshine. Israeli soldiers are guarding the proceedings, standing on the walls with machine guns watching the entrance from the Hinnom Valley. The participants in the last scene are to enter the cemetery and proceed on the path leading to Schindler's grave. Each is carrying a stone which will be placed on the grave of Oskar Schindler, in accordance with Jewish custom.

They are coming, walking by the tomb, each taking a moment to place their stone. Danka Drezner from Israel and her film counterpart, Ania Mucha, a Kraków sixth-grader. Jonas Drezner and Maciek Tajber. Henry Rosner from New York, violinist from the well-known Kraków musical family, and Jacek Wójcicki. Henry Rosner's wife Mancy and Kraków actress Beata Paluch. The son of Henry and Mancy, Olek Rosner—a well-known computer specialist who came from the United States with his exotic wife—and his film counterpart, four-year-old Kamil Krawiec. Henry's brother Leo, from Australia, and Piotr Polk. Niusia Karakulska's brother, the prominent New York photographer Ryszard Horowitz, is walking alone. His film counterpart, Michel Babiarz from Kraków, did not come. Two days earlier while taking a bath he was overcome by carbon monoxide from the water heater. Fortunately he was saved. When one portrays a person who survived Auschwitz, one can count on a special Providence.

Still they come: Mila Page from Los Angeles and Adi Nitzan from Israel; Mila's husband Leopold "Poldek" Page (Pfefferberg) and Jonathan Sagalle from Israel. Rebecca Tannenbaum and Beata Nowak from Kraków. Helen Hirsch, whom Oskar Schindler won in a card game from Amon Goeth, and Israeli actress Embeth Davidtz. Marta from New York is accompanied by an Italian actress, Beatrice Macola, who played Ingrid in the film. Mrs. Emilie Schindler has difficulty walking. She is in a wheelchair pushed by Caroline Goodall. Mrs. Stern, widow of Itzhak Stern, Schindler's "right hand," is holding the arm of Ben Kingsley. They are followed by three hundred others. Each places their stone on the tomb and retreats to the shade of the cypress trees by the wall of the cemetery. After the filming, David James takes a group photo of the participants standing around the tomb. In the center of the group stands Liam Neeson with Emilie, surrounded by the Schindler Jews. Everyone is moved to tears as much as Steven Spielberg, who after the end of the scene could only say, "It is so moving."

Spielberg is thanking everybody for taking part in making the film and for coming to Jerusalem. There is the last-minute signing of autographs and saying goodbye to the actors. The children who were in the film take their time. Ania Mucha puts her arms around Steven's neck and whispers in his ear for a long time. Agnieszka Makuszewska finally interrupts, asking for an autograph. The director writes her a souvenir: "To Agnieszka, who is more beautiful than Julia Roberts.—Steven Spielberg."

The actors have finished their assignments, but Spielberg is asking the living Schindler Jews to walk with him onto one of the hills surrounding Jerusalem because he wants to film one more scene: They all should walk together standing next to each other in a single row, facing the camera. This is a parallel to the scene which was filmed the last day in Kraków. On a hill in Jerzmanowice, one of the villages near Kraków, a group of prisoners just liberated from Brinnlitz was walking through the field of fresh wheat; it was a beautiful scene. As I watched then I sensed an echo, a resonance with moments in the films of such great European romantic drectors as Wajda, Bergman, Clément, and others, in which life is affirmed amidst an open grassy field. Now, two days after filming the actors in that scene, the real Schindler Jews are walking over the hill in Jerusalem.

After the first not-so-successful try they are asked by Sergio to try to walk in an even single row, and together. One of the Schindler Jews says in jest, "Who ever saw Jews marching in unison? Every one is an individualist walking to his own inner rhythm." Every one is his own Moses, as it was beautifully said by Sholem Asch.* It is very true of this group. Maybe that's why they survived. After a few tries, Spielberg is finally pleased with the take and thanks them one more time.

"God bless you," are his last words on the set of *Schindler's List*.

[TRANSLATORS' ADDITION: Franciszek Palowski had not seen the film when he wrote this book. The film hd not been released when the book was published. So Mr. Pawloski was not aware of exactly how these takes made for the ending would actually appear in the film.

For the film, this final dramatic scene achieves an extraordinary concluding moment in cinematic storytelling and for the audience of this film. The liberated Schindler Jews walking through the field are seen in black-and-white. As they walk the full image takes on color for the first time since the beginning of the film. As the image resolves into color, we become aware that the people walking over the field now are older, in contemporary clothes, and smiling and walking in a different spirit. Then we realize we are seeing the Schindler Jews as they are today—alive and well. It is an image of overwhelming affirmation and confirmation.]

---

*Sholem Asch (1880–1957) is a Yiddish author who came from eastern Europe to the United States in 1910. He gained an international following through novels and plays that took a warm, genial, and sensitive look at Jewish folk and life.

Every one of the Schindler Jews received $22 for his or her part in the film. All those honorariums were gathered together and given to Emilie Schindler. Her part in rescuing the Jews during the time in the Brinnlitz factory is not fully appreciated. The tree honoring Oskar Schindler and planted by him at Yad Vashem grew with a split trunk forming a V. Poldek Page said it was symbolic. The letter V is a symbol for victory—victory of good over evil. According to Poldek, this double trunk, the only one in Yad Vashem, calls attention to the fact that there should be another plaque under the tree—one of the special plaques placed to honor the "Righteous Among the Nations of the World." That plaque should be in the name of Emilie Schindler.

Immediately after the last take, Spielberg got into the car with his wife, Kate, for a ride to Ben Gurion Airport in Tel Aviv and an eighteen-hour flight to Los Angeles, where their children were waiting. We say goodbye with a wish: "Till we see one another in a year—at the Oscar ceremonies in Hollywood."

The rest of Steven Spielberg's actors and crew returned to the Catholic Cemetery on Mt. Zion. There, on a small square shaded by a grove of olive trees, a group of students from a Jerusalem school provided refreshments. It was the last opportunity to take a look at the Hinnom Valley, the site of the ancient burning of innocent victims—a place so deeply affecting human consciousness that "Gehenna" is still a symbol of hell and suffering, though thousands of years have passed. In more recent time it is the pyres of the Holocaust that burned—and such a pyre was lit in Steven Spielberg's film.

That took place on Saturday, a week before the director left Kraków. Not far from the cloister of the Benedictine fathers in Tyniec, but on the opposite side of the Wisła River, a seven-foot high pyre of human bodies was built. Of course the bodies were made out of plastic. The scene to be filmed was the burning of the bodies of the victims executed in the Płaszów camp and other Kraków prisons. The bodies had been buried in a deep ravine within the camp. As the Red Army was approaching, every effort was made to liquidate and cover up any proof of the

German crimes. In the last month of 1944, tens of thousands of bodies were burned.

Simon Wiensenthal, famous for having devoted his life to finding Nazi war criminals, recalled the event in 1996 while he was in Kraków to receive an honorary doctorate from Jagiellonian University. During a new conference, I asked him about his impressions of the *Schindler's List* film. He answered, "Do you remember the scene when Jewish prisoners had to exhume bodies of executed Jews in Płaszów?"

"Of course I remember," I answered.

"I was one of them," he said, "—those real prisoners in the Płaszów Camp. This was a terrible job. When we came back to camp we stank so terribly the other prisoners would not let us into our barracks. We had to sleep outside. And there was one guard of Austrian origin who commanded our work detail. He was a cruel taskmaster, and from time to time he punished us for nothing, only because in his opinion we were too lazy. One day I promised myself that if I survive, I will find him— however long it takes. I knew his name; I knew he was Austrian.

"After the war I asked someone who was a linguist, a specialist in the regional 'signatures' of names, if by chance there is in Austria a specific region where we can find people with such a name. Yes, there was. I started to look for this man and found him. He was growing roses..." So it was that Simon Wiesenthal's dedication to become the "Nazi Hunter" was born out of his experience in Płaszów Camp—a prisoner forced to labor at erasing the "testimony" of the dead.

Back in 1985, I filmed a documentary at the site of the former camp in Płaszów. After finishing the film, I suddenly noticed a small corroded metal object lying on the side of the road. I reached for it. It was a carbine bullet. There were others, and some used shells, too. I rubbed the bottom of a shell on the asphalt path; the name of a German manufacturer appeared. We wondered where they came from. Poldek Page recalled the spot as a place where pyres for burning the exhumed bodies had been set up. It is possible that the bullets were imbedded in the bodies and that after the burning they stayed to bear witness to the tragic past.

Years later, Allan Starski and Michał Szczerbic are preparing such a pyre on the shores of the river among the limestone boulders. They have constructed a conveyor to transport the "bodies" to the top. Even the weather aids in the gloomy atmosphere. A thunderstorm is approaching; dark clouds are gathering in the sky. There are thousands of "skulls" and human "bones."

The scene cannot be rehearsed because the fire is real and the pyre will become smaller with each take. Five cameras are ready—two will film in color and three in black-and-white. Spielberg, Janusz Kamiński, and all the assistants are behind the cameras. A special-effects expert starts the fires. The heat can be felt far away. Even though I look from behind the camera and can see it is not real, the view is terrifying. Geysers of flames rise sky-high with the help of bottled gas inside the pyre.

Steven, however, is not pleased. The flames resemble the burning oil wells during Desert Storm. "I do not want the war with Iraq." He decides to repeat the take from a greater distance using large telephoto lenses. The fire is to be put out and everybody must get ready for a repeat.

A hundred yards away is a fire truck. Not far from it a small boy is catching tadpoles in a little puddle. The fire truck pumps water from the river to douse the pyre. Clouds of steam rise. By then the black clouds have moved on to hover over Kraków, and the sun now shines over Tyniec. Suddenly a rainbow appears over the pyre. It lasts but a few seconds. Noah's ark comes to my mind. "I do set my bow in the cloud," said God, lighting the rainbow in the sky after Noah landed the ark on Mount Ararat and made a sacrificial fire, "and it shall be a token of a covenant between...me and you and every living creature of all flesh: and the waters shall no more become a flood to destroy all flesh." Never again would God set upon the earth such a cataclysm.*

The ark, I thought. It is no exaggeration to regard that achievement as similar to what Schindler did in rescuing those Jews.

*Genesis 9:13–15.

13

Conversation

I was promised this interview would take place during Spielberg's second visit to Kraków in June 1992, but it did not materialize because of the director's very intense schedule. Spielberg reassured me then that when he returned to Kraków in three months there would be a lot of opportunities for interviews. In reality, the matter of scheduling was very complicated. Daily work on the set lasted until evening, then Spielberg worked at his residence, editing. I did not dare to even mention his promise to me.

At the end of March, Anna Maria Stein announced, "It has been decided, you will get an interview." Anna Maria was officially in charge of publicity and was the only person employed in the production of *Schindler's List* who could arrange press visits on the set and any contact with Spielberg or actors in the film. One time I asked Jerry Molen, with whom I am quite close, if I could interview him. I was thinking, if I had a direct line to the source, why should I use a go-between? His answer, however, was, "Talk about it with Anna Maria." Then I understood that in this precise system one has to present a particular request to the person directly responsible for the matter and paid to do the job. From then on I never tried shortcuts.

During the filming of *Schindler's List* about three hundred members of the press and several television productions wanted to come to Kraków, visit the sets for the film, get interviews with Spielberg and his major stars. Some directors feel that the presence of mass media on the set during filming is necessary. Steven Spielberg is not among them. He prefers to create without publicity and the eavesdropping of the curious. Only when a work is finished should it be seen and judged. Anna Maria told me that during the making of *Jurassic Park* (which is already a greater success than *E.T.*) no one from the press was allowed on the set. In the case of *Schindler's List,* Spielberg agreed to relax his rules, but only for the most prestigious publications, including, among others: the *New York Times, Life, Newsweek,* the *Los Angeles Times*; and from Poland, *Gazeta Wyborcza* and *Rzeczpospolita*; and two or three newsmen from Israel and Australia.

Anna Maria Stein scheduled my interview with Spielberg for Monday, April 5, two days before a scheduled press conference, but later the schedule was in a state of confusion because of an unexpected heavy snowstorm. The press conference was called off and it never materialized; the time and date for my interview also had to be changed. My problem was that we already had scheduled the TV broadcast for Easter Sunday, before a higher power had taken over. Now, in the worst case, the Easter Sunday interview would have to be canceled.

The final scheduling of the interview was determined by chance. An opportunity to bring up the topic occurred a week earlier, on Palm Sunday. It was during filming of one of the key scenes on the hill of St. Benedict on Krzemionki, when Schindler and his girlfriend Ingrid go horseback riding. Poldek Page and his wife Mila had come to the set. During their conversation with Spielberg they asked me to join them, so I took the opportunity to ask him for a date for the interview.

"Whenever you want it."

I proposed doing it during a break for lunch.

"Could the interview be taped in black-and-white, just like my film?" he asked.

"Of course."

We finally scheduled it for Good Friday. That way we still would have at least a bit of time for editing and translating for the Sunday broadcast. It was not exactly my dream schedule, though. Also, I thought it would make an especially interesting background to use a part of the set, with maybe some extras. On Thursday Spielberg was to begin filming small scenes in the TV studios in Łęg where a replica of the Montelupich Prison and the interior of the Amon Goeth villa were built. There was nothing to discuss, of course, if one had to choose between an interview or no interview. I went to Łęg on Thursday. In the studio there was a replica of the Goeth villa with a huge terrace which I thought would be the best place for an interview with Spielberg. I was hoping that the Master would agree to our use of two cameras. There was not much reason to hope, though; Anna Maria had said that he had never agreed to that before. I did not give up. Using Bonnie Curtis, Steven's secretary as the go-between, I showed her my dream space and asked her to convey to Spielberg my request to use two cameras. Bonnie returned after a few minutes: "Steven agrees to the terrace and the two cameras," she said.

I proposed fifteen questions. Probably too many, since I was told I would have twenty minutes into which to squeeze everything. It was not possible to make the interview longer. Any more time would cause a delay in the production, requiring an additional day's pay for everybody. The rules for work bow to the strict regulations of the American unions—and there was no magic act that could trick their watchful eye.

Friday the shooting started at 8:30 A.M. Steven arrived on the set twenty minutes earlier. Our talk would take place between 1:00 and 2:00 P.M. I wrote each question on a separate card; that way it would be easier to change a sequence of questions or eliminate some. A question should not be so constructed that one can answer with just a single yes or no. One question I wanted to ask I had been carrying around for half a year. I wrote it in New York, when I was inspired by a ten-year-old article I had found about Spielberg.

Around noon, during a short pause for changing the lighting in the interior of Amon Goeth's villa, I had an opportunity to talk briefly to Spielberg. I related to him the themes I wanted to touch upon in our interview. He had no objections. Some diplomacy is still needed, however. We talk to each other on a first name basis, of course—the American way—but for television should I refer to him as Mr. Spielberg? I consulted with Anna Maria and Jerry Molen. "Absolutely not," they both agreed, "you refer to him only as Steven." Well, it would be on Polish television—it might sound funny to be so familiar. Until now it has been unheard of in Poland for even the best of friends to talk to each other on television using the familiar "you." They pretend that they have met for the first time and refer to each other as Mr., or Mrs., or Miss. It has been changing more recently, but not everybody accepts it and some consider such familiarity especially inappropriate behavior for a newsman. I was sure I would be accused of impropriety, but I could just see Steven's face when I referred to him as Mr. Spielberg. On the other hand, many of my viewers would be offended if I skipped the formalities. Well, that's too bad. I choose to omit the "Mister."

The morning of filming lasts longer than scheduled. The break is at 2:00 P.M. Spielberg has left for a short time to relax. He will return in ten minutes. We take the opportunity to change the setting. The wicker chairs which were used in the film are replaced (they have a tendency to crackle during conversation). Steven Spielberg will sit in his signed director's chair. I use one of the chairs marked "Actor." This proves a good omen.

The video equipment for the interview is installed, but at the last moment we discover someone had locked the studio door through which Spielberg is supposed to make his entrance. With some quick legwork and a bit of luck, we get it open on time.

Jurek Jędrzejczyk and Romek Piotrowski are my cameramen. We have known each other for years. Twenty years ago I made my first TV interview, with Jurek working the camera. He was then an assistant to Wiesiek Kielar, whom I later interviewed. Kielar was prisoner number 290 from the first transport to Auschwitz and is the author of the well-known book *Anus Mundi*. So, by working with Jurek on camera again my television career comes full circle, returning again to the war theme. Maybe it is a sign that it is time to say, "That's enough." André Gide once said that journalism is the most wonderful profession in the world, under one condition—that someday one calls it quits. Now may be that moment. After all, for a journalist, an interview with Spielberg is tantamount to a mountain climber's conquering Mount Everest; even then, after all, another eight thousand difficult summits remain to challenge the daring. I console myself with that thought.

Spielberg is dressed in his jeans and a soft comfortable jacket. I am very tense. Just a moment ago Branko Lustig asked me if I was nervous.

"Awfully," I answered.

"It's not necessary. Everything will go well," he encouraged.

I am still very tense when Spielberg and I sit down on the terrace and I ask my first question. Then Steven gives me a friendly smile and my tension disappears, as if removed by the simple wave of a hand.

FRANCISZEK PALOWSKI [F.P.]: When I requested this interview, you expressed your desire to have the interview filmed in black-and-white, not in color. Why was that?

STEVEN SPIELBERG [S.S.]: Well, because *Schindler's List* is in black-and-white—it's the first movie I've ever made in black-and-white. It was a decision that I was hoping you would agree

agree with. Everything about the movie—the subject matter—is so historically in black-and-white. I thought it would
be representative of the film we are making to even do the
interview this way.

F.P.:   So is it the first black-and-white movie you ever made,
even counting the first one made, when you were twelve years
old?

S.S.:   No, I made all my movies in color. I did, but some of my
favorite classics are in black-and-white.

F.P.:   I have heard that long before you even thought of being a
film director you had a profound experience at your grandmother's house that became a part of your consciousness and
which inspired you to undertake this subject. I mean, the
problem of the Holocaust.

S.S.:   When I was about three years old—and I can only give
you the age because my parents remind me how old I was
during this part of my childhood—we lived in Cincinnati,
Ohio. My grandmother, on my mother's side, taught English
to Jewish immigrants from Poland, Austria, and Germany.
All of them were survivors of the Holocaust. There was a long
table in our dining room, I recall, and she'd have many
people, my mother told me almost forty, three days a week
around this table learning how to speak English. My grandmother would teach them. How they immigrated to Ohio
from Eastern Europe I have no idea, but that's where they
wound up. I remember vividly a man at the table who taught
me to recognize numbers. I had never learned numbers
before. I didn't know a "2" from a "5," I didn't know a "9"
from "1," I remember very vividly how he rolled up his sleeve
and showed me the numbers tattooed on his forearm. I
remember how he showed it to me: "Look, that is a '2,'" he
said. "That's a '5'; that's a '7,'" and then he said, "I'm going to
do a magic trick for you." I'll never forget; children love and
remember magic tricks. He said, "Look," and pointed to his
forearm. "This is a '9' but if I do this," he bent his elbow, "the
'9' changes to a '6,' and when I do that," he straightened out

his arm, "it is a '9' again." I just have this image that I'll always remember the rest of my life of the "9" and the "6"; the "9" becoming the "6," the "6" becoming a "9." It meant nothing to me as a child, but it was a memory that stayed with me. Only later, when I was old enough to understand what had happened between 1936 and 1945, did I understand the significance of that experience in my life.

F.P.: John F. Kennedy once said that the United States is a nation of immigrants. He even wrote a book under such a title.* The group of immigrant Jews you met at the age of three exemplify President Kennedy's thesis. From where do your ancestors derive?

S.S.: My ancestors come from two groups. Some of my maternal ancestors come from what is now Poland but was Austrian territory, others come from Russia. So we're part Russian and part Polish.

F.P.: If you consider that Kraków is a Polish town which belonged to Austria, and that not far to the north was a border with Russian-occupied Poland, if your ancestors did not immigrate to the United States you could be a Krakovian.

S.S.: I could. I feel very much at home here, surprisingly. This is not a foreign country to me.

F.P.: When did you first come across the Oskar Schindler story?

S.S.: I had never heard of Oskar Schindler. I had heard of Wallenberg [a Swedish diplomat who rescued Jews, and who after the war disappeared into the Russian gulags.] but I had never heard of Oskar Schindler. I remember that one day Sidney Sheinberg, who is, and was at the time, the head of Universal Pictures in Hollywood, sent me a book review from the *New York Times* reviewing the Thomas Keneally novel, *Schindler's List*. I read the book review, was fascinated with the story—just based on three pages of review—and based on

---

* John F. Kennedy, *A Nation of Immigrants* (New York: Harper and Row, 1964.)

that I read the book. Then, based on that, Universal bought the rights in 1982 for me to film the novel. That's how I came across the Oskar Schindler story.

F.P.:   When did you decide to make the film?

S.S.:   I had the rights to make the film eleven years ago, actually. I didn't go to work on it right away because I didn't know *how* to do it. The story didn't have the same shape as the films I have made. It certainly is not an entertaining story in the way I make entertainment. It was something that didn't come naturally for me. A subject like this wasn't as easy for me as it would have been for Andrzej Wajda. This was much more difficult, and I needed more time—and in the 1980s I started to build a family, to have children. I needed time to mature within myself and develop my own consciousness about the Holocaust. I had to wait until a time when I really felt that I was ready to express myself on the subject of Oskar Schindler and make a very serious movie about his life and deeds.

F.P.:   *Schindler's List* was published in 1982. That same year *E.T.* premiered, breaking all box-office records in the history of film. The more I think about *E.T.*—I viewed it again recently—and *Schindler's List,* the more there appears to be similarities between the two. In a philosophical sense, both films deal with the necessity of understanding something foreign, to love it despite racial and cultural differences. Could you comment on this theory?

S.S.:   Well, the traumatic events in the life of Elliott, the little boy in *E.T.,* result from his parent's recent divorce. He is in great need of a companion; he needs a father figure in his life, and E.T. fills that need, coming into his life just when he needs a friend.

But *Schindler's List* is based on a tragic explosion of murder, tears, and sorrow. It is about an entire world in woe—in grief caused by a horrible, horrible series of inhuman events. I can't make the comparison in my own mind; maybe I'm too close to both films. In my own mind I can't make the comparison between *E.T.* and *Schindler's List* because I've never approached material like *Schindler's List* before. To me it's a completely different kind of experience than I've ever had as a filmmaker. I've never told a story like this—such a serious story.

F.P.:   *Schindler's List* is also different from all your other films in the sense that until now your creative imagination was more important in your work than facts. But *Schindler's List* has sometimes been labeled a documentary film. How much room is there for your creative imagination—which we recall is a trademark of yours—in a film like this?

S.S.:   I feel like more of a journalist than a director of this movie. I feel like I'm reporting more than creating. These events, this character of Oskar Schindler, and the good deeds he did at a terrible time weren't created by me, they were created by history. I'm sort of interpreting history, trying to find a way of communicating that history to people, but I'm not really using the strengths that I usually use to entertain people. I have a very strong urge to entertain, to keep the audience interested—not to bore anybody. Now, to make this movie, I am using a completely different set of tools that, as a filmmaker, I never really had my hands on before. This film is not supposed to please an audience—bring the audience to an exciting, adventurous conclusion. Life is not a film. In this sense, this film resembles life much more than life would remind one of film.

F.P.:   I found the following quote in a *Time* magazine from ten years ago [May 31, 1983]: "He is a child at heart. Inside E.T. are the feelings of a little boy. That boy is thirty-four-year-old director Steven Spielberg. *Time* took a closer look at the movie-making genius to explore the special sensitivity of a man who can reach the child in all of us." In *Schindler's List*, are you also searching for our better part, trying to find the child in our souls?

S.S.:   I don't think so. It seems, rather, that I am searching for the souls of all the children who were murdered as a result of what *Schindler's List* is about. This film isn't really celebrating anything having to do with the child in all of us; it's not even meant to communicate to that little person inside of us. This movie is much more a remembrance—a way to stimulate the memories of people so they just will never forget the Holocaust. In that sense, this movie is not for children or about children. It is really a film about and for our own personal consciousness—conscience and consciousness.

F.P.:   I have had the honor of being able to watch you work on this film from the beginning. I am really moved by the whole crew's incredible dedication and the enthusiasm with which they work. How would you explain that?

S.S.:   Well, I think we all realize we are doing something very important. I think we all feel we are making a contribution— not just to the movies—but we're making a contribution toward the world remembering the Holocaust. I think everybody realizes that this isn't just another movie. We hope people view this film, but even if they do not see it, it will become part of the record—the public record—about the deeds of the Nazis between 1936* and 1945. In that sense we have all bonded in an effort to communicate something that we feel is of great importance.

F.P.:   In your company there is a substantial group of Polish actors, such as Andrzej Seweryn, Henryk Bista, Beata Rybotycka, Jacek Wójcicki, Beata Paluch, and Aldona Grochal, among others. There are other Polish artists as well. For example, I am thinking of Allan Starski, the production designer, and the production crew, led by Lew Rywin from the Polish film studio Heritage Films. How would you assess their role and input in the making of *Schindler's List*?

S.S.:   Well, when I came here, I came with a little trepidation because I had only worked with crews from Britain or America. I had never worked with anyone from other countries; I did not know or appreciate the dedication of the crews

---

*Hitler actually came to power in 1933, but he became an international threat in 1936 with the remilitarization of the Rhineland.

from Poland. When I arrived to begin filming I was surprised—and I continue to be surprised and amazed—at the dedication and efficiency of the Polish crews. This is very important to me because I like to get in a lot of shots every day. We have been averaging twenty-five to thirty different camera setups a day. That's more than I get in the United States or in England. Thus far this has been the most productive amount of work achieved on a daily basis in my experience—and this is my twelfth feature film as a director. I have never experienced this kind of fast, efficient, and very organized production. This is amazing to me.

F.P.:   I couldn't be a Krakovian if I didn't ask you how you like living in Kraków and what your family who accompanied you here think of our city?

S.S.:   My four-year-old son Theo told me after only three weeks in Kraków, "Dad, you know, I like Poland better than Los Angeles." I said, "Why do you say that, Theo," and he just said, "Well, it's different and the food is better." That was his opinion. We have had a good time here. You have to understand that I'm looking at this city as a stage. A stage that we didn't have to construct. We didn't build anything except this rare set in the Łęg studio and the Płaszów camp set in the Liban quarry. Everything else is filmed in existing locations and mostly where the events of the story actually happened. Krakow has made us a gift of its history and opened up its history books to us to let us dance through the pages of their history to make this movie about what happened here. This place fascinates me. Every time I turn a corner I say, "Could Schindler have walked down this street? Was Amon Goeth around that corner? Is this where he drove his car when he divided the ghetto into ghetto A and ghetto B? Did he stand here when he sent people from the ghetto to labor and extermination camps?" One can smell the scent of history on every corner. I am in a restaurant and some one casually tells me that this restaurant is six hundred years old. In America, nothing is six hundred years old; well, no—maybe the Grand Canyon.

F.P.: I would say the Grand Canyon is more like six hundred million years, if not more.

S.S.: Exactly, but going back to Kraków, nothing here was destroyed by the war. People were stunned and struck down emotionally by the Nazis and then they were paralyzed by the Communists. So this city has survived a horrendous fifty-year ordeal which luckily is coming to an end. I look forward to Kraków and the entire country of Poland enjoying a full and total recovery—both spiritually and economically.

F.P.: On the set during filming you have met and still are meeting some of the real life heroes of your film. How did they influence you?

S.S.: Well, it's unusual to be making a film on the streets where the events actually happened and to have a woman come over to me as a woman did a couple of weeks ago. She said, "I was an eleven-year-old Jewish girl working in Oskar Schindler's DEF, Deutsche Emailwaren Fabrik. I wished him 'Happy Birthday' on behalf of all the workers in the factory, and he gave me a kiss on the cheek. For that kiss he was sent to Montelupich Prison, accused of breaking the rules of racial purity." To actually meet this very lovely sixty-one-year-old woman, who at the time played a vital role in the life of Oskar Schindler, was a wonderful experience, and this is not the first time this has happened to me. I've had people come up to me on the streets to say, "I was a Schindler woman"; "I was at Emalia"; "I was in Płaszów camp"; or "I went to Brinnlitz." It's just incredible to meet the people from that former time who are still here—the people whose stories we are telling in this film.

F.P.: One of them is Poldek Page (Pfefferberg), our mutual friend who inspired Thomas Keneally's creating of *Schindler's List* and is one of the heroes of your film. He tells me each time I see him that it will be this film, about Oskar Schindler, that will bring you that much-deserved Oscar from the American Academy of Motion Picture Arts and Sciences. I wish with all my heart that this will come true.

Thank you for this interview.

s.s.:   Thank you.

For a long time I hesitated about whether I should mention the Oscar award. The fact remained that for this man, who twenty years ago was considered a wunderkind of Hollywood, who revolutionized the film industry, attaining one success after another, not to have received the prestigious Oscar was probably trying to Spielberg's soul. His films were awarded Oscars for editing, special effects, and so on, but Spielberg himself had never received an Oscar for directing. In 1975 he was nominated for *Jaws*; he lost to Milos Forman, and *One Flew Over the Cuckoo's Nest*. In 1979, *Close Encounters of the Third Kind* was pushed aside in favor of Woody Allen's *Annie Hall*. In 1981 Warren Beatty's *Chariots of Fire* won over *Raiders of the Lost Ark*. A year later *E.T. The Extra Terrestrial* was defeated by Richard Attenborough's *Gandhi,* and *The Color Purple* (1985), which had a near-record eleven nominations, did not receive even one Oscar, losing to *Out of Africa*. In Hollywood it is a joke that the reasons for this strange restraint among the members of the Academy toward Spielberg are the "three *S*'s: success, special effects, and Spielberg."

By creating films which are an immediate success with the audience, Spielberg destroys a certain myth about the creation of films: that success is something extraordinary, that one has it rarely, only from time to time. In the meantime, Spielberg has had continuous success for twenty years. It is a great source of frustration for some. Spielberg's situation is reminiscent of the case of another wunderkind of Hollywood, Orson Welles. He, too, was passed over by the prestigious members of the Academy that awards Oscars. Some critics think that the prime reason behind an Oscar not having been awarded to Spielberg is the fact that he does not make films dealing with serious themes. Well, let us wait a few months for the premiere of *Schindler's List*.

Taking into consideration his previous losses in the Academy Awards, it was somewhat tricky to wish Spielberg an Oscar for *Schindler's List* at the end of our interview, but the mood at the time was intimate and open, so I decided to wish him an Oscar for Oskar Schindler.

One of Steven Spielberg's personal characteristics is his incredible power for dramatizing an idea. When he told about the incident from his childhood, he rolled up his shirt sleeve and actually demonstrated the trick of changing the "6" into a "9," and vice versa. He gesticulated with animation and laughed when he talked about his adopted son Theo, who prefers Poland to Los Angeles. What's most important, he did not let me feel even for a moment that there was any distance at all between him—the film genius invited to presidents' homes—and a modest journalist with whom he was conversing. There is nothing about him to suggest that he is a great star, though it is a fact. Again and again I am convinced that true greatness is like that. Therefore, to emphasize that characteristic of Steven Spielberg I allowed myself to translate the English *you* into the Polish familiar form—*ty* ["thou"]—for our interview when it was telecast in Polish.

A souvenir of our talk was a photo of the head of the ugly Extra Terrestrial which I cut out of *Time* magazine. The photo was taken by Steven Shapiro and paradoxically titled "Human." Steven Spielberg wrote on the picture: "To Frank, whose heart and faith in us all will never be forgotten."

Epilogue

by Robert G. Ware

When we consider the circumstances this book documents, we realize that the appreciative autograph Steven Spielberg wrote to Franciszek Palowski on that *Time* magazine photo of E.T. was not at all gratuitous. Time and the film itself have confirmed that Palowski's faith in Steven Spielberg was well placed.

The filming for *Schindler's List* was completed in May 1993, and immediately that fall the original edition of this book was published in Polish. The film itself premiered several weeks later, in December 1993. The author's enthusiasm for the promise of Spielberg's efforts was based on having observed and worked with the director throughout the whole filmmaking process in Poland. What he had seen by just observing the filming of the script led him to believe in Spielberg's potential for crafting a great film from that raw material. Palowski's foresight with respect to Steven Spielberg's achievement in making the film was amazingly accurate.

When the world began viewing *Schindler's List*, it became apparent that this was a singular cinematic achievement. Despite the serious and often shocking content, audiences were compelled to participate in its drama. Many were moved beyond most other film experiences they remembered. In the newspapers and the trade papers, the pre-Oscar awards talk speculated: Would now be the time Steven Spielberg would get his Oscar for directing?

Oscar nominations were announced. Heads turned as the entertainment world realized that this film about perhaps the most horrific inhumanity in history had garnered twelve nominations—two short of the record. Then came the awards themselves: seven Oscars, including Best Picture of 1993, Best Director, and Best Cinematography. Ironically, the Oscar for Best Cinematography had gone to a black-and-white film the studio wanted made in color, believing that today black-and-white had no commercial potential.

While irony is at the heart of all good drama, it was another sort of irony that distinguished Spielberg's achievement with *Schindler's List*: audiences were being captivated by this riveting dramatization of one of modern humanity's most repugnant episodes. Their discovery, through that experience, was that this film was a drama that ultimately engaged them in a celebration of all that is best about humanity—the capacity to gloriously survive adversity whenever even one soul decides to confront evil. In *Schindler's List* audiences discovered a film that celebrates the potential in the mere moral effort to survive, and celebrates it modestly—in black-and-white. The film actually succeeded at what Spielberg had set out to do: draw the attention of a major audience throughout the country, and soon the world, to a new awareness about past injustice and the true nature of simple heroism—righteousness. With this film, Spielberg managed to establish a gratifyingly simple recipe for being heroic—follow the Golden Rule. Heroes do not prevail only by strength in numbers or muscle. The first requisite for a hero or heroine is to be morally right—right, not might. David versus Goliath.

The uniqueness of Steven Spielberg's achievement is that he managed to capture history in a form that entertains as it instructs—a quality Aristotle saw in the best dramas of his time—the classic Greek tragedies—and an element we find in the best drama today. Spielberg's accomplishment is to vividly immortalize an element of recent history that exemplifies the *essence* of intolerance. In the days of silent film, D. W. Griffith explored this same topic in films such as *Intolerance* (1916), but he drew upon the broad scope of recorded human history to convince his audience intolerance exists.

Slowly we have come to understand that those Greek tragedies Aristotle honored so highly were not simply sad, depressing stories of great people who lose their lives. Rather, those great dramas celebrated the highest possibilities of human endeavor, possibilities of such value that the greatness of heroes was measured by their daring to risk their own lives—to expose their own imperfections or flaws—in order that society might survive. Griffith's awesome effort presented us with images of human intolerance made arresting by showing the suffering of victims in juxtaposition to the opulent spectacle of the idealized, insensitive lifestyles of their oppressors. Griffith's focus on his subjects, however, does not offer the tragic possibilities inherent in Spielberg's story. Griffith leaves it to his audience to react to what he reveals, and to go out and pursue their own efforts at change. Spielberg's drama has a hero, Oskar Schindler, and he presents him to us as a revelation about the power of a single, imperfect, but righteous human being to suppress intolerance in his own corner of the universe. Spielberg fascinates us through the audacity of this ordinary opportunist whose conscience leads him to risk all to save a few. He takes the experience of one group of people from one moment in time to astonish us both with inhumanity and humanity—and to celebrate the triumph of the human spirit.

The medium for both of these twentieth-century masters of film is black-and-white—Griffith by necessity and Spielberg by choice. In their art, however, each reveals that intolerance is one of the few areas of human experience in which there can be no "gray" area. Intolerance is a stark issue. To conquer intolerance is what restores the color to our lives and the joy to our spirit—a fact made manifest by Spielberg in his film with a remarkably controlled and, for him, uncharacteristic understatement. Seldom in today's world of media frenzy, glitter, and excess do we find an artist with the courage to follow the axiom, that "less is more." In *Schindler's List,* Spielberg makes economy and control of every resource a great artistic asset. This book has allowed us to become intimate with some of his processes and his inspiration.

Spielberg's choice to tell this story in black-and-white was a conscious artistic decision. One might think this had to do with his plan to make a controlled use of color. Franciszek Palowoski reports, however, that Spielberg's mind was on the issue of the story itself. He viewed the subject matter as only suitable for black-and-white because it is about the denial of humanity, about an effort to annihilate the soul of a people. At the end of chapter 8, for example, Spielberg is quoted as saying to Poldek Page, "The Holocaust...was life without light. For me the symbol of life is color. That's why a film about the Holocaust has to be in black-and-white." In chapter 13, in the conversation with Franciszek Palowski, Spielberg reminds us that the historical record of the Holocaust itself is in black-and-white—the newsreels of the liberation of the camps, the Germans' own historical photographic and motion picture records. Beyond his own imagination and impressions, however, there is another long established aesthetic simply in the conventions that accrued from the aesthetic and impression set upon the world by all the powerful films of the twenties, thirties, and forties. It was in acknowledgement of this that Sir Laurence Olivier chose the medium of black-and-white for filming his famous and well-regarded production of Shakespeare's *Hamlet* in 1948. Then *Time* magazine (June 28, 1948) noted that Olivier had made *Hamlet* in black-and-white when everyone who could afford to was using the new, but expensive, Technicolor process for their major work. Only a few years before, Olivier himself achieved major artistic success using Technicolor for his acclaimed masterpiece, Shakespeare's *Henry V*. Olivier chose black-and-white deliberately because of its capacity to engage an audience more vividly with the inner drama of the characters—the issue was not external spectacle but rather internal clarity. Two great artists, one of theater and one of cinema, both deliberately use black-and-white film to convey dramas of intense personal character.

However Spielberg may have come to this vision, the fact remains that his decision gave him additional dynamic dimension for cinematic creativity. The vivid quality of the black-and-white medium gives strength to the images of inhumanity. On the few occasions that color comes into the film, those moments gain strength of another kind—suggesting the vivid vitality of the human spirit. The film's first image is in color—the lighting of the candles for the traditional Friday evening service to begin the Sabbath. We see the family group in a warm glow, but in moments the glow of a single candle burns down to a faint red-yellow dot in a nearly dark field of gray black—and extinguishes, its dying gray smoke taking us into the black-and-white world of the Nazi occupation. Later we see the red coat of Genia, that little girl who ignited Oskar Schindler's interest in saving what Jews he could. Still later, when Goeth has been ordered to exhume and burn the ten thousand Jewish dead from Płaszów and the ghetto, her memory appears to return as the corpse of a little girl in a reddish coat passes by Oskar Schindler atop a cart of bodies on its way to the pyre at Chujowa Górka. Then, after the move to Brinnlitz, Schindler invites the rabbi to hold the first Friday evening service since their captivity; this time only the candle flame itself glows with color— the warmth of life has begun to return to their spirits. Finally, as we note near the end of chapter 12, there is that great moment when those liberated, younger Schindler Jews striding freely across an open field becomes a color scene of the survivors walking across the Jerusalem plain in 1993—a breathtaking sequence that creates a soaring sense of joy in the spirits of all who watch. Without the dynamic contrast of having the black-and-white world against which these moments can play, their value to the drama Spielberg is relating would be diminished. It is filmmaking such as this that is at the core of the cinematic greatness that draws us into *Schindler's List*.

The interest of audiences in the film continues. A major precedent was set when *Schindler's List* was first shown on television. On Sunday, February 23, 1997, NBC telecast the film complete in its entirety. It has been reported that sixty-five-million households viewed it that evening. More importantly, however, NBC agreed to show it uninterrupted by commercials. There were commercials, of course, (eight minutes worth); but they were all presented *before* the film began. American television had not telecast without commercial interruption for that length of time since the assassination of President Kennedy.

The year 1993 was an unprecedented one for Steven Spielberg. In addition to the premier of *Schindler's List,* it was also the year *Jurassic Park* was released. That film set box-office records and itself won Academy Awards for Best Sound, Best Sound-Effects Editing, and Best Visual Effects. After two such record-setting films in one year, what does one do next? Be very careful, or selective, for one thing. Forget about topping yourself, for another.

After *Schindler's List,* Steven Spielberg did not work behind the camera for three years. *The Lost World: Jurassic Park,* the sequel to *Jurassic Park,* opened on May 23, 1997. Spielberg did principal filming between September and December, 1996. *The Lost World* is probably among the last films to come out as a joint project of Universal Pictures and Amblin Entertainment. This is because in 1995 Spielberg joined forces with two high-powered colleagues, former Disney Chairman Jeffrey Katzenberg and record and film producer David Geffen, to create a new production company, DreamWorks SKG. Spielberg has been busy putting this major enterprise together. He has produced some films, probably read some new scripts, doubtless spent quality time simply as a father—and planned.

Four years after making *Schindler's List,* he is once again engaged in breaking new ground and again making motion picture history. Having drawn the attention of the world to the Holocaust both for its horror and its promise, Steven Spielberg has turned his creative energy to an infamous moment in the history of black slavery in America. As this essay is written, he is currently in postproduction on *Amistad* which, like *Schindler's List,* is due for a December premier. This new film is the story of a shameful but true incident in the United States of 1839. Captive Africans on an illegal slave ship bound for the United States overpower and kill their captors, save for the captain and mate. In exchange for their lives, these two agree to take the kidnapped "captives" back to West Africa, from whence they came. Deception, characteristic of human exploiters every-where, results in these miserable, displaced Africans, who have no understanding of English, being taken to Long Island. There they are taken prisoner and put on trial for the deaths of the smuggling slave-ship sailors they killed in their mutinous strug-gle for freedom. *Newsweek* (April 7, 1997) already hints there may be reason to compare this new film effort to Spielberg's achievement in *Schindler's List.* First, obviously, because of the historically significant subject matter, but there are other groundbreaking reasons they cite, as well as a few they likely would not have known about before the publication of this book. Somewhere in all this there may be some keys—some actions or decisions, deliberate as well as coincidental—to Spielberg's preeminence.

Consider for a moment some parallels in Spielberg's recent production work. Before he could begin *Schindler's List,* he had to finish filming *Jurassic Park.* While filming *Schindler's List* he was doing final editing on *Jurassic Park.* Four years later, in December 1996, he had finished filming *The Lost World: Jurassic Park.* While that film was still in its final production and editing stages, in February of 1997—the same month in which he began shooting *Schindler's List* four years earlier—he began shooting *Amistad. Amistad* finished shooting in May, as did *Schindler's List,* and is scheduled to premier in December, completing the parallel in scheduling. As was the case with *Schindler's List,*

Steven Spielberg has made what will likely be another dramatically compelling film about another profoundly disturbing event of human history. For *Amistad,* Spielberg is collaborating with many of the same persons who worked on *Schindler's List.* Steve Zaillian, who wrote the script for *Schindler's List,* has also written the script for *Amistad.* Janusz Kamiński is again Spielberg's director of photography, and Michael Kahn his editor.

As Spielberg broke ground by filming *Schindler's List* in its historical locations, and daring to make a film in black-and-white when no major film has been made in black-and-white in years, he now takes another daring stride, but into different territory, with his newest film. The subject matter of *Amistad* is drawn from the African-American slave experience. The conventional perspective of the African-American community has been that no one but blacks could make an authentic artistic work about the black experience. Recently, this argument has been hotly sustained by public debates both in print and in the lecture hall between the playwright August Wilson and the drama critic Robert Brustein (Town Hall, New York, January 27, 1997). Quietly, Steven Spielberg forges new territory as he shoots this film. Collaborating with the best artists, critics, historians, and producers from the black community, Spielberg makes film history as he creates the new work. From all reports, he is bringing a new vision to another drama of disturbing, searing inhumanity that somehow causes the indomitable human spirit of its victims to soar above the source of their pain. If what Steven Spielberg accomplished with his vision and ability to control his medium in *Schindler's List* gives us any indication, then for a second time we are about to be treated to a film that further challenges all preconceptions of the distance entertainment must keep from reality if it is to capture an audience today.

At this writing, *Jurassic Park* is the all-time highest grossing film worldwide. For its opening weekend in May 1993, *The Lost World: Jurassic Park* set new records. While critics generally expressed disappointment that Spielberg did not outdo himself with this sequel, the critic Terrence Rafferty, writing in the June 2, 1997, *New Yorker,* lauds the director for his genius at self-satire, exposing the shallowness of the monster movie genre itself as he dazzles us with his spectacle of fantasy. In general, however, the critical press is more interested in *Amistad.* What Spielberg's achievement will be in that project cannot yet be known. *Newsweek* (April 7, 1997) takes the view that Spielberg is a different director now, post–*Schindler's List. Premier* magazine for May 1997 quotes Spielberg as saying that he will not direct another sequel to *Jurassic Park,* though he might serve as its executive producer. Speaking of how making *Schindler's List* changed him, Spielberg says that while making *The Lost World* he discovered he was "growing more and more impatient with myself with respect to the kinds of films I really like to make." He says that after making *Schindler's List* he promised himself that he would not just make films like it, either. He confided to Peter Biskind, author of the *Premier* article, that he would like to make a love story and had a secret desire to direct a musical. Whatever the outcome, it will be exciting to look back from some future moment at what these new films will reveal about his current artistic development.

Soon after this book is published, it will be time for another Academy Awards ceremony. Then we will regard Franciszek Palowski's book about the making of *Schindler's List* as a glimpse at what may prove to have been a major turning point in Steven Spielberg's creative life.

A FINAL NOTE

Where are the Schindler Jews today? Amongst all of European Jewry there were some 6,000 of them and succeeding generations of their families living in all parts of the world at the time the film was made. Several still spend time speaking to groups and working in schools to confirm their experiences and give history the vibrancy of their presence. Leopold "Poldek" Page has closed his retail store but continues the wholesale portion of his leather goods business. His weeks are punctuated with requests for appearances from around the world and he travels to fulfill as many of these as he is able. He continues as a leader of the effort by survivors of the Holocaust to engage in educational and charitable enterprises—living testimony to the difference individuals can make in insuring a better world for our future generations.

MAJOR AWARDS FOR *SCHINDLER'S LIST*

Academy Awards

12 Nominations; 7 Oscars Awarded (Awards are in boldface.)

Best Picture of 1993: *Schindler's List*
Best Director: Steven Spielberg
Best Actor: Liam Neeson
Best Supporting Actor: Ralph Fiennes
**Best Screenplay Based on Material Previously Produced or
    Published: Steven Zaillian**
Best Cinematography: Janusz Kamiński
Best Editing: Michael Kahn
Best Sound: Andy Nelson, Steve Pederson, Scott Millan, and
    Ron Judkins
Best Costume Design: Anna Biedrzycka-Sheppard
Best Art Direction: Allan Starski and Ewa Braun
Best Original Score: John Williams
Best Makeup: Christina Smith, Matthew Mungle, and Judy
    Alexander Cory

British Academy Of Film And Television Awards

Best Director: Steven Spielberg
Best Film of 1993: *Schindler's List* (shared with *Shadowlands*)
Best Supporting Actor: Ralph Fiennes
Best Writing: Steven Zaillian (shared with *Groundhog Day*)

ABOUT THE AUTHOR

Franciszek Palowski—journalist, television producer, and writer—lives in Kraków, Poland. Born in 1942 in the small Silesian village of Skrbeńsko, he undertook studies of Polish language and literature in 1963 at the oldest and most prestigious university in Poland, Jagiellonian University of Kraków. While still a student, he began his journalistic career as a freelance writer, graduating with honors in 1968. For the 1971–72 academic year he was a visiting scholar at the Columbia University Graduate School of Journalism under a grant from the Kościuszko Foundation.

Upon returning to Poland in 1972 he accepted a position with the Polish Television Network in Kraków. Beginning as a reporter, he soon became the anchor of the local news program, then its producer, and, finally its editor in chief. His documentaries have been aired by the Polish Broadcasting Network, the Polish Television Network in New York City, and various networks in France and Germany.

During one of his visits to the United States, Franciszek Palowski met Leopold Page—the Schindler Jew who inspired Thomas Keneally to write *Schindler's List*. Palowski produced a documentary about Leopold Page and they became close friends. When Steven Spielberg first traveled to Kraków in 1992, Franciszek Palowski served as his guide and interpreter, and later as a consultant on the film.

Franciszek Palowski completed his Ph.D. at Jagiellonian University in 1992. Now an independent producer, he is also an interviewer for the Steven Spielberg Shoah Foundation and works throughout Europe helping to gather the oral history of the Holocaust.

During his thirty years as a journalist, Franciszek Palowski has received numerous awards and honors. Twice the Kościuszko Foundation selected him for grants to study abroad. The United States Information Agency invited him to lecture and study in the United States on two different occasions, and the Polish Journalists Association has twice named him laureate for his journalistic achievements.

INDEX

191